THE EMPOWERED COMMUNICATOR

THE EMPOWERED COMMUNICATOR

7 Keys to Unlocking an Audience

CALVIN MILLER

BROADMAN
& HOLMAN
PUBLISHERS

Nashville, Tennessee

4211-44
0-8054-1144-5

Dewey Decimal Classification: 251
Subject Heading: PREACHING // PUBLIC SPEAKING
Library of Congress Card Catalog Number: 94-1951

Scripture quotations are from the
King James Version of the Bible.

Library of Congress Cataloging-in-Publication Data
Miller, Calvin.
    The empowered communicator: 7 keys to
    unlocking an audience / Calvin Miller.
        p. cm.
    Includes bibliographical references.
    ISBN 0-8054-1144-5
    1. Preaching. 2. Laypreaching. 3. Public speak-
    ing—Religious aspects— Christianity.
    I. Title.
BV4211.2.M48 1994
251—dc20   94-1951
                                     CIP

Acknowledgments

The first and best part of my thanks always goes to Barbara, my companion in every venture of consequence.

I must offer my hearfealt thanks to three people. First of all, I am grateful to you, son Timothy, for being so everlastingly patient with me as I have tried to learn the world of computer graphics. Second, to you, Michele Rice, I appreciate your work. In spite of your busy life as a student, you seemed to see this manuscript as a project of love. Your commitment to the book so often kept me on track. Third, to you, Todd Holt, my faithful student assistant and reader, I will ever be grateful. I know your studies were demanding and yet you always seemed to find time for this manuscript.

Table of Contents

Introduction

Holding an audience without a rope is the all-consuming art of every preacher in this current age of communication. There are seven all-important keys to this elusive art, and ignoring even one of them will leave a speaker frustrated by audience disinterest. Without these keys, the preacher will find that the sermon remains locked. Those who need the message will be locked out of its motivating truth. This book is written for all preachers who, much more often than we would like to admit, live Sunday by Sunday in that locked-out world.

With this ring of keys, however, preachers can persuade congregations to give them the most splendid gift any audience can give a speaker: their attention. All congregations usually understand that preachers live for audience response, but the Christian world has become terribly chatty, ever making speeches. Sermonizing has become cheap because it is done so frequently and often poorly. Every church speaker has some agenda to sell, and every assembly has some reluctance to buy. We have listened so much to preachers that we have learned to listen reluctantly if not skeptically. Every religious audience has become a gathering of question marks.

- Who is this speech for?
- What evidences do I have that my attention will be rewarded by authentic counsel and relevant content?
- Whose agenda is really being promoted—mine or the speaker's?

This fortress of audience doubt, bolt by bolt, locks listeners behind high walls of silent skepticism. Unless the Christian persuader can unlock this skepticism, the gospel message is lost.

Throughout this volume I will use interchangeably words such as *preacher*, *teacher*, and *communicator*. Of course, I hope this book will keep in touch with the best principles of all communication. But it is specifically directed to preachers and other Christian communicators who want to sharpen their communicative skills.

Perhaps the toughest question the Christian communicator faces from church-goers is this: Does anybody here speak for God? The words of the Christian communicator must be, "Yes, here I am! Listen! Count on my integrity. I have studied to make this speech relevant to your life. You may trust me." But our claim to integrity must be more than a sworn statement. Our honesty needs to become believable in the delivery of our communiqué. Declaring too forthrightly that we are completely trustworthy only calls the issue into doubt.

The preacher's integrity must come from spiritual authenticity. At the outset of this book, this principle must be laid down: *Any claim of knowing God is pointless unless the speaker is really acquainted with God.* This dimension of inner authenticity proclaims itself naturally for those who "practice the presence of God." This inwardness should never be referred to; it must be that silent undergirding of soul which cannot help but proclaim itself. Even unspoken, such devotion will be the loudest part of our proclamation. Our speech is only what we *say* we are; our inner life in Christ is what we *really* are. Emerson said that what we *are* stands over us and thunders so loudly that others cannot hear what we *say*. Every communicator's authenticity arises from inner and genuine "is-ness" to establish the force of "says-so."

Furthermore, what is said must clearly communicate that we are Christians who speak for Christ. As the speech develops there must not be one sentence or one word which causes the hearer to doubt the force of our inner life in Christ. This is the Christian communicator's Isaianic sign. Isaiah, in his call experience, protested. He felt he could never be the kind of communicator God was calling him to be:

> Then said I, Woe is me! For I am undone;
> because I am a man of unclean lips, and I
> dwell in the midst of a people of unclean
> lips: for mine eyes have seen the King,
> the Lord of hosts.
>
> Then flew one of the seraphim unto me,
> having a live coal in his hand, which he had
> taken with the tongs from off the altar:
>
> And he laid it upon my mouth, and said, Lo,
> this hath touched thy lips; and thine
> iniquity is taken away, and thy sin purged.
>
> Also I heard the voice of the Lord, saying,
> Whom shall I send, and who will go for us?
> Then said I, Here am I; send me.
> Isaiah 6:5–8

To be a Christian communicator is to sense that our own lips have been cleansed for a strategic kind of communication. God calls us to more than a special rhetoric: we have a special reason to be. Only when we understand this will our message come across as God's agenda. Hearers must sense that our communication has been purged by live altar coals. Only then will they believe that we do not speak *our* words for *our* benefit but *His* words for *His* benefit. God commends Isaiah and sends him out to communicate with these words: "And he said, Go, and tell this people, Hear ye indeed, but understand not; and see ye indeed, but perceive not " (Isa. 6:9).

When the audience senses that the preacher has heard God say, "Go and tell this people," they will yield their whole attention to the herald. This is all-important, for without the gift of their attention, the keys of communication unlock nothing. The use of these unlocking principles must always be preceded by this axiom: The power to communicate is a power which is conferred not seized. The Christian communicator's power comes from two possible sources: It is conferred both by audience interest and by visitation of the Spirit.

Communicating on Conferred Power

Living in the communication age, we cannot help but be bewildered that so many sermons are muddled and unclear. Sermons often seem to be the least-communicative form of contemporary speech. How did this happen? Considering the sheer intensity of their importance, it is odd that sermons seem impotent.

Consider where the Christian sermon was born. Sermons from the Book of Acts can only be characterized as oratories of power. By contrast, consider the truth of this modern cliché: "The clock struck twelve on Sunday, and the church gave up her dead." A kind of communicative *rigor mortis* stalks contemporary worship. How did it happen? The wind-and-fire communiqué of Simon Peter at Pentecost should call the church to regain all that it has lost.

Communication derives historically from a glorious passion, one that changed lives and world destiny. Such a vital heritage ought to quicken the church and call her to reclaim her lost birthright. What is missing these days? What has gone wrong?

The word "power" in the New Testament most often derives from *dynamis,* from which we form our words *dynamic* and *dynamite*. Communication in the New Testament era was assumed to be a communication of power. No other kind of communication had occurred to the church. To speak for the all-powerful Christ is to speak in power. So when we speak of power in this book, we are in no way trying to stroke the self-importance of baby boomers. Power should be the expected mode of communicating the gospel just as it once was. If *power* as an adjective now seems out of place, it may only serve to illustrate how much of the vitality of contemporary sermons has been squandered on the non-vital subject matter of today's preaching.

Most evangelicals agree, at least in theory, on this issue of power. God confers it on the sermon as the primary source of the speaker's vitality. God's conferred power is what makes Christian communication Christian. Only when Christ's Spirit fills both the preacher and the sermon does God's involvement inhabit preaching.

How could first-century communicators hold audiences with mere sermons? Sermon power in the New Testament was not a force that speakers contrived from clever techniques, studied theology, or rehearsed phraseology. After all, the early church was void of biblical commentaries and illustration books. Yet sermonic force was seen to devolve upon the communicator. This force came as Spirit to empower the text. Power created crowds and called unbelievers to faith. People thronged around the speaker's spiritual passion. Have the centuries somehow eroded the communicator's power? Could it be because they once came to church to hear lives. Why are they now content to merely hear sermons?

Be warned at the outset of this work: If you want help in learning to produce sermons for selfish ends, this book is not for you. If you conceive this volume as a how-*to* book on crowd-manipulation, you will be disappointed. This book is committed to *dynamis* communication—power from God for any purpose that God may wish to use to accomplish His ends in His world. God confers no power to enhance our audience clout or reputation. We must proceed on the assumption that God wishes to give this power only to men and women who are committed to His agenda.

The Spirit of God is the first source of power for the sermon. The other source of power is the audience. Audiences cannot be forced to listen. Listening is a "group grace" that listeners extend to speakers. The audience aspect of power communication is less impressive than spiritual power, but it is no less important. Many books on the indwelling work of the Spirit can teach us the disciplines by which we may become heirs to this spiritual *dynamis*. So, to begin, let us ask ourselves what we must do to deserve or earn the audience's ear. How do we motivate audiences to grant us this power?

Power Granted Only After Trust Established

The sermon's entire argument rides on the rails of trust. Character invites trust, but character is often unknown when preachers themselves are unknown. Knowing the speaker makes character assessment possible, so preachers who address the same audience every week have a chance to build this reputation. But what of those speakers who are unfamiliar to us? To be heard, preachers who are unknown to an audience will have to develop "instant reputation." Such instant confidence says, "You should trust me even though you don't know me." How can this happen? What makes an audience listen? What causes that trust?

Trust is the *sine qua non* of all communication, as the rhetoric of civil elections makes abundantly clear. The slogans of past presidential campaigns cried out for viable political platforms. Warm sloganeering always lobbied for trust: Roosevelt's New Deal, Kennedy's New Frontier, Bush's Family Year all said, "Trust us." Sometimes these slogans asked for personal response—Goldwater's "In your heart you know he's right" or Eisenhower's "I like Ike." In one way or another, the world of communication always lobbies for trust. A preacher must communicate that, in effect, the audience can trust him for three reasons:

1. He has been asked to speak by someone whom the audience does trust. That recommendation of him should give the audience confidence in what he says.
2. Every new relationship can only proceed from a generosity of spirit that places openness above skepticism. In effect, every unknown speaker says, "I am at your mercy in this matter of trust. Won't you please presume that I am authentic, until further knowledge of me can authenticate your opinion?"
3. Because an audience cannot try his sermon against his unknown character, it should try his words against other truths it already endorses. What it thinks of "all" truth paves the way to a

fuller trust of "his" truth. The preacher says, "My message is His message. I am but the medium through which His message proceeds. Listen generously and uncritically until the message certifies the medium."

There is some truth in Marshall McLuhan's adage that the medium is the message. But in another sense the message usually precedes the medium. That is, people hear our words before they get the chance to assess our character. Our deportment and delivery must say, "Let your acceptance of my words pave the way to your acceptance of me." Moses made integrity the principle. He said, "When a prophet speaks in the name of the Lord, if the thing follow not, nor come to pass, that is the thing which the Lord hath not spoken" (Deut. 18:22). The believability of sound words makes the person who speaks those words believable.

In a later chapter we will examine the power that comes from the Holy Spirit. But much of the *power* of power communication is granted by those who hear it. Generous people, therefore, are also a source of our power. The argument which follows in this book will depend on this doubled axiom: both spiritual power and audience-conferred power must be in place if preachers are to make any significant differences in their audiences.

With these two essentials in mind—spiritual power and audience power—let us proceed with the seven bases of communication. May these seven keys, with rehearsal and maturity, bring you to the status of power communicator. Resist the word *power* if you are tempted to see power as audience control rather than effective speech. This book will have failed if it gives you some Genghis Khan desire for crowd manipulation. It will have gloriously succeeded if it lures you toward the noble calling of a servant communicator. The power of servanthood will then be for you a mode of preaching the whole counsel of God. And after all, God's counsel is the *only* legitimate business we have to transact with any audience. This counsel distinguishes the Christian communicator from all other kinds. Power communication is always servant communication.

Key One:

Building a Speaker-Listener Relationship

First rehearse your song by rote,

To each word a warbling note.

Hand in hand with fairy grace

Will we sing and bless this place.[1]

The Audience Challenge
of
Key One

Dear Speaker:

I would like very much to hear what you have to say. I am afraid, however, that my attention is locked to all who want to speak to me but have no desire to know who I am.

I am a person with all kinds of needs. As a listener I am aware that you are being paid to speak to me, while I am paid nothing to listen to you. Actually, you are one in a long line; during my life I have listened to many speakers. Most of them never knew I was in the crowd. I had needs back then; I still do. I still carry around a lot of the same emotional luggage I carried in those bygone days. It was heavy then. It still is.

I know you want me to listen to you. I will begin to do it, as soon as I sense that my needs are more important to you than your words. I am plagued with fears, but I promise to hear you the moment you help me feel secure and unafraid. I will listen when you prove to me that you can help me by wrapping my anxieties in peace.

Your speech will never reach my ear until your eye has seen me as I really am.

I am loneliness waiting for a friend.

I am weeping in want of laughter.

I am a sigh in search of consolation.

I am a wound in search of compress.

If you want to unlock my attention, you have but to convince me you want to be my friend. When you make me feel like I am the only person in this vast audience, I will give you what I have given to very few: the unbroken focus of my mind.

—Your Audience

Communication is an interchange of thought from the mind of a sender to that of a receiver. The sermon event is a drama of three parts: the sender, the medium, and the receiver.

We have already defined the sender as a Christian, someone who believes in Christ and is committed to His agenda for the world. The medium is, for the overall purpose of this book, a sermon, speech, or lecture. The receiver may be any audience with which God has a specific agenda.

The Communication Triad

Sender ➡ Medium ➡ Receiver

The Preacher   The Sermon   The Hearer

Relationship Is Everything

William Shakespeare had Mark Anthony challenge the Romans: "Friends, Romans, Countrymen." Obviously, Mark Anthony was good at audience analysis, but he was even better at communication theory. "Lend me your ears," he said.[2] Mark Anthony was well aware that nothing could be communicated until he had established a speaker-listener relationship. Indeed, establishing a speaker-listener relationship is the first key to communicating. Before we examine how this is to be done, a cardinal principle must be addressed: the matter of first impressions.

First Impressions

Before we who preach are ever introduced to an audience, our hearers have already been trying to make up their minds about us. Their assessment always comes before our words. Our deportment—the way we walk, sit, stand, and our facial expressions—all are a part of what is called first impressions.

These first impressions really begin, not with the audience's visual rating of us, but with the much more intrinsic issue: How do we preachers see ourselves? Our self-concept is probably most obvious, radiating outward from all our hidden notions of who we are. Four things, says communicator J. Michael Sproule, cause our hidden self-concepts to emerge:[3] First, we discover who we are as we measure the reactions of others toward us. Second, our real selves show through as we react to others' expectations of us.

Four Ways to Locate Our Self-Concept

1. **Audience reactions toward us**
2. **Our reactions to the audience**
3. **The comparison of ourselves with those we address**
4. **How comfortable we feel with the situation we address**

Our ego-defensive mechanisms begin a process of self-justification. Third, we define who we are by comparing our strengths and weaknesses with those around us. Finally, we demonstrate how well we perform under pressure when we gain or lose control of our situation. In other words, under pressure we discover how competent or incompetent we are.

A preacher I once heard became enraged by a teenager who kept running up and down the aisle during his sermon. He finally lost control and showed obvious anger. He blew the cover off his weak ego. He lost his highly prized self-esteem. His procedures spoke of his character, and his hearers were disgusted by his arrogance. The pressure of his communication matrix revealed the sort of man he really was.

Bob Schuller notes, in such books as *Self-Esteem: The New Reformation,* that evangelicals are the group in America with the lowest self-esteem. This low self-esteem often leaks out in public speaking situations. All Christian communicators would do well to work at self-analysis and self-improvement. The more we know about who we are, the more consistently we will be heard.

First, audience evaluation often begins with such simple issues as how we dress. Is our dress properly selected? Is it finished but not gaudy? Have we pressed the wrinkles and shined our shoes? Every potential listener will have a slightly different definition of what "well dressed" means; nearly all, however, will see our clothes as a significant part of their first impression.

Second, how is our personal appearance? Our nails, our hair, our makeup? These things also stamp our right to communicate as acceptable or unacceptable.

Third, our deportment is also a part of the big picture. Do we strut, swagger, dawdle, or pace? Do we smile, scowl, look droll, or frown? All these communicate impressions before we ever stand up to preach.

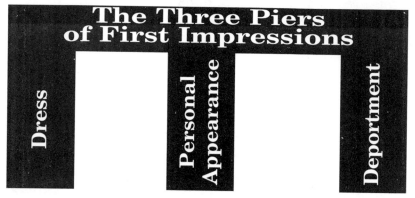

The Three Piers of First Impressions

Dress — Personal Appearance — Deportment

How important are first impressions? Believe it or not, non-verbal impressions determine whether or not people will even listen to the sermon. If they decide to listen, the hardest part of our work is done. If they decide not to hear us, we will have considerable work to do to bring them back across the wide gulf of negative first impressions.

Again, J. Michael Sproule reminds us that listeners quickly note our facial expressions, which display feelings such as contempt, surprise, disgust, joy, and anger. All these are measured and our inner person is silently catalogued in their minds. In 1975, Elkman conducted some experiments with New Guinea aborigines. Natives were given a set of three facial photos and told three stories of Caucasian men and women. These natives were able to match faces and emotional narratives 95 percent of the time.[4] First impressions do matter.

I remember picking up a church staff interviewee at the airport. Having made a lifetime study of the dowdy way that preachers are prone to dress, I instantly spotted the young man as he was getting off the plane. He was overweight. There was dandruff on his colored shirt, the tail of which was flagging unbelted. His pants billowed creaseless above his scuffed shoes. He did smile, but his none-too-white teeth proved only to be the gateway to an incredibly active halitosis. Had he the talent of John Chrysostom, he would not have been able to move me to call him as an associate. His talent later proved as undeveloped as his hygiene.

However, poor first impressions may be overcome. I also remember an equal and opposite case. Another preacher who came to speak to our church made a similarly poor first impression. His dress and deportment were slouchy. His rhetorical style was "stumble-bum." But no matter. His communication skills—many largely natural—were so effusively warm that after a few minutes, we forgot our first impressions and sat captive to his performance.

There are no charm courses for the preacher-communicator, but a book like *Dress for Success* is sometimes worth its weight in relationships. Also an honest counselor can advise us on how to get the offense out of our offensiveness. We are often the last to suspect the extent of our unkempt impression. Learning to listen to others' critiques can be all-important, yet the best insight to monitoring our first impressions is developing our own critical eye. The mirror is a harsh but honest counselor. Usually the more critically we learn to inspect ourselves, the less critically we will be seen by others. The mirror is a good place to study our dress and deportment. It is also a good place to rehearse our communiqué. Preaching to mirrors reduces how we think we appear to how we actually appear.

The First Three Minutes

Reg Grant and John Reed suggest that an introduction to a thirty-minute sermon should usually
take about three minutes to set the stage.[5] I agree,
and I want to suggest two or three ways to use these
first three minutes. Ours is a relational day and age.
Keep this in mind as you ask, "What can be done in
the opening minutes of a sermon to make relational
contact with the audience?"

There are two kinds of gigs that must hook the
audience in the opening moments of a sermon. The
first is relational: People listen to speakers they
relate to. The second is the subject: People listen to
subject matter in which they have some interest. The
wise communicator, wherever possible, begins by
hooking listeners with both gigs at once.

The Trust-Interest-Content Continuum

First Impressions
(How I appear to you)

The Speech Before the Speech
(Getting to know you)

The First Three Minutes
(May I have your attention?)

What I Came to Say
(Here's why you need to listen)

The first three minutes before an audience determines whether or not they will hear us at all. This is particularly true with college and younger-aged groups. If their attention is not snagged in the first three minutes of a presentation, it will be nearly impossible to gain it back. Therefore, the first 180 seconds are the most critical moments of our whole communiqué. How may we best use this time to snag audience interest in our subject? The answer lies in four areas. Let us turn our attention to the first of these.

The Speech-Before-the-Speech

Our communication begins before our formal talk. Beginning a sermon well is to hide its early agenda in informality rather than formality. In almost every instance of hearing someone give a splendid speech, the splendor is owed to that casual, sometimes sauntering start wherein the speaker warms up to the audience. Apart from any of the substance of the speech, the speaker may tell a friendly story. He or she may say something complimentary about the audience or their town or the occasion that brings them all together.

True, these remarks will not be remembered like the subject of the speech itself. We draw the dramatic quotes of Churchill or Roosevelt, not from their opening remarks, but from the body of the speech. Yet their opening remarks, at the time, established a strong audience rapport that formed the relational matrix of their quotable content.

When President Kennedy spoke to the New England dairymen about the all-important (to them) subject of price supports for New England commodities, he opened with the now famous lines, "As the cow said to the milk-maid in February: 'It's nice to have a warm hand on a cold morning!'" The remark may seem a trifle corny but as an opening remark it was relational. It was his talk-before-the-talk.

In a church setting, this talk-before-the-talk is all-important! Here the elements of worship that preface the sermon may be splendid. The choir, soloist, drama club, or testimony can be used as a springboard to establish the relationship which connects the subject of the day to the audience. But the talk-before-the-talk can do much to establish the audience relationship. This pre-sermon talk avoids going too directly to the formal beginning. This round-about course is the getting-to-know-you stage of the sermon. Not much can happen until friendship is fixed, and the first words of the sermon are the "fixing" place. Because this phase of the sermon is rarely written down, it may seem to the preacher to be unimportant. The actual truth is that, written or not, it is the most human thing that may be said.

Many popular writers and scholarly thinkers agree that 1950 was the magic year that the age of communication began. Coinciding with that era, sociology and psychology became a part of the relational age. We are now at the zenith of the communication age. Are not the lounges and bars of our age temples to our exaltation of relationship? The virile loneliness and isolation of the corporate world is beckoning the church to true community.

Why is all of this important? Because *formality* is a stifling word, and *casual* is an endearing word. Every television show these days seems to be either a talk show or an easy sit-com that includes the audience in its sense of community. TV shows prove that we want our entertainment to be relational and all-inclusive. On these talk shows, the audience's needs, interests, and cultural literacy are never violated. Isn't this spirit quite obvious in television journalism? Even the news is done round-table fashion. All three anchorpersons gather around a centrum to discuss sports, weather, and world events in a jocular and friendly fashion. Everything from great disasters to upcoming blizzards is anchorperson chitchat. Earthquakes and mass murders are coffeeklatch journalism.

Audience question #1: Do I like this speaker? Perhaps only in formal churches is there a rigid adherence to older forms that stifle community and the conversational style. Should such situations exist in an age of relationship? The talk-before-the-talk provides a formality-smashing, relational foreword! Why? Because in this crucial warm-up time the audience is answering some basic questions about the preacher. What does this preacher really know that can help me? Will he preach against my lifestyle? Is he or she a fuddy-duddy? A prude? An egghead? Most important, do I like this person?

The Communication Matrix
Stepping Toward Your Audience

The Non-Communication Matrix
Stepping Away from Your Audience

Audiences rarely feel love at first sight toward a preacher. They have to be given a reason to feel *like* and *don't-like* toward the person who is asking for their attention. The sermon subject is not what engenders this *like/don't-like* polarity. It is this seemingly unrelated opening sermonic chatter that wins or loses their ear.

Remember Maslow's hierarchy of human needs—self-actualization, esteem needs, belongings needs, safety needs, physiological needs? The talk-before-the-talk accosts the person at the level of his or her belonging needs. These words that precede the sermon form an early relational step of identity. The humanity of the speech-before-the-speech says upfront, "Before I get to my sermon, I want you to know how we're alike. We are all human. We have the same needs. You can listen to me comfortably for this reason."

I remember the story of an Arizona parson who faced an outdoors service on a hot, strangling day. Nobody was in the mood for a sermon in the sweltering desert heat. The good reverend said, "Considering eternity without God, don't you agree that the day is hotter than hell?" It was the closest that the good reverend had ever come to swearing. He didn't quite swear, but the near-profane remark from a preacher drew them in and made them laugh. He intersected their sense of identity and belonging. His sermon was not long, and that was smart of him. But his sermon was well attended because of the words that came before the Word.

On Super Bowl Sunday, it is sometimes appropriate to say a word about football. Everyone is thinking about football anyway. Such remarks generally lie within the realm of all that is human. No wonder Emil Brunner once said that to be an evangelist you must first be a human being. Could anything be truer? Since real people like listening to real people, the first moment of our speaking should convince them that we are real. The first words we say should appear to come from a genuine fellow-struggler.

Audience question #2: Does this speaker like us? After they ask themselves if they like the speaker, audiences will ask, "Does the speaker like us?" How are preachers to make audiences feel they are loved? Somehow preachers must use their first words to dispel the myths that audiences hold in their minds. What are these myths?

- Preachers make a lot of money.
- Preachers are know-it-alls.
- Preachers travel all the time and never really see anybody.
- As soon as this preacher gets the honorarium, he'll be on his way.
- All preachers are egotists.

Humanity dispels these myths. What is the real message of this warm-up time? It can say, "I like you, and here's why." But be careful! Compliments are effective, but flattery embarrasses. In the long run, excessive flattery leaves a speaker less credible.

One final aspect of audience rapport that may work but should be used advisedly is *self-depreciation*. Remember Sam Ervin's consistently referring to himself as a poor country lawyer during the Watergate hearings? In referring to himself in this diminished way, he drew the people of America closer to him. John Denver's classic song, "Thank God I'm a Country Boy," won him a great hearing even as he devalued his urbane mystique.

But what are the pitfalls of self-depreciation? It can have a ring of insincerity about it. It makes the speaker appear humble (and that is a positive), but it also may make a speaker appear dishonest. Somehow Sam Ervin's Harvard mystique showed through his mock humility. John Denver's poor-country-boy status cannot hide the fact that he is a multimillionaire. Self-deprecation should be used sparingly.

The Critical Warm-up

If you are a guest preacher, be generous. Take enough warm-up time, especially before the first sermon in a series. You need extra warm-up time if you are a visiting speaker for a series of sermons or lectures. Why is this first sermon so important? Because it gives your listeners enough trust in relationship that they will grant you the power you need for all the later exchanges.

What does this same principle say about the local pastor who may have stood for years before the same congregation? Is this warm-up time as important when the talk-before-the-talk is not necessary to establish trust? Mark this: the warm-up may be shorter but it is still necessary to retain an essential humanness if long pastorates are to endure. This is especially true in static smaller congregations. Preachers who rush into their subject matter are likely to come across as coldly prophetic. But isn't the status of a prophet a good thing? Yes, but it is also risky. Beware of a prophetic mystique within a small community. A little fun time, a relational start, can help preachers not take themselves too seriously. It can also help the congregation to see their pastor as a real human being. Human beings live better in community than do prophets.

Three Issues of Relationship

Here's How I'm Like You!

The first issue of audience identification is the question, "How are we alike?" Again the preacher's genuine sincerity must not yield to some bogus identity. A Baptist speaking to Presbyterians might warm up to his audience by mentioning his Presbyterian roots. Of course, he should do this only if he has Presbyterian roots. In speaking to farmers, it is honest to mention your years on the farm, only if you once lived on one. But where you can honestly touch the listener's roots and lifestyle, it can serve the issue of identity.

In these crucial words before the sermon, we are trying to establish identity. It is still true for the most part that audiences are not sitting there crying out, "Give me information for my deliverance!" Much of the time (and this is especially true in younger audiences) they are crying out, "Tell me who I am! But please, start by telling me who you are." Most of the time they are not crying out, "Motivate me to do something I don't want to do! I long to be convinced that I ought to die for Jesus in Africa!" Rather, they are asking, "Feel my condition before you speak to me. Emote with me

Three Questions for Establishing the Communicative Relationship

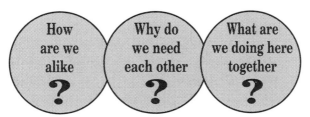

before you instruct me. Understand me before you teach me. Show me how we're alike. If you do that well, I'll hear your agenda later."

I have been a preacher for thirty-five years. I think I have always tried to preach a biblical message and, to paraphrase Lincoln, the world has little noted nor long remembered. But I think some people do remember my identifying with them and my participating with them in the community. In the classroom, I have heard the cry of a new generation of lonely students. Many current theological students have risen to education, often out of the ashes of their single-parent culture. They enter the classroom crying, "Don't teach me today; just sit with me. May our need for oneness displace our need to learn. May our cold anonymity be dissolved in liquid humanity."

Coupled with their need for identity, these students also have an open disregard for burdensome content. "Don't get heavy, man!" is the body language of today's younger audiences. The world says "Don't lecture me" and "Don't preach to me." This rhetoric is not anti-intellectual at its heart; it is a cry for understanding and genuine identity.

Still the preacher needs to preach a word of significance. The sermonic word must originate out of a need to make the homily a content document. So as soon as we leave our conversational beginning, we must move to a *content of vitality*. This content must apply to our listeners' lives in ways that they consider important. To preachers, the content of our sermons is our reason for being, but we should resist the temptation to rush headlong into heavy argument. However important it may seem to those of us who preach, our content will be less important to most of our hearers than our togetherness.

Here's Why We Need Each Other!

It is difficult in this pre-introductory part of the sermon to speak to the issue of needing each other. Still, this issue is key. In addition to establishing audience identity, we also must tell the listeners *why* we need each other. This is particularly true when our sermon topics have been announced well ahead of time. When our listeners know what the subject matter will be, they may or may not be eager to hear it. We must ask ourselves how we can best present our material for their profit. What about the case of the Sunday sermon with text and title listed in the bulletin? Wouldn't it be good to include a word about why this subject was chosen? In the case of an announced academic lecture, shouldn't we designate some time to explain why this series will be useful?

Whatever is said by way of pre-introduction, it should be said in a modest manner. In other words, how can we avoid saying it as though we are going to enlighten them? How can we refrain from intimating that only our superior understanding will enable them to live a full and meaningful life? Induction allows listeners to rule on sermon application. Good inductive procedure leaves the onus of acting on the sermon as a congregational responsibility. Induction values the listeners. It endows them with a judgment equal to the preacher's. Good inductive style warmly tells them of our desire to make them worthy conversationalists in the unfolding dialogue. We assure them that we are eager to enlarge our own insights. We want to learn from them even as we teach them. G. K. Chesterton once said (and this should be the emotional backdrop to every sermon), "We are all in one small boat on a stormy sea, and we owe each other a terrible loyalty."

Here's Why I'm Here!
Here's Why You're Here!

The speech-before-the-speech is an exercise in audience bonding. How else can we let listeners know why we think it is important that our minds should meet? Even when advance publicity has already stated the purpose of the sermon, the pre-sermon should issue a call for our being together. It may also be a time of letting them know what they may expect to receive as they listen.

How about issues of promise and fulfillment in the pre-sermon? It is a good thing not to begin by promising more than the speech can deliver. Never tell the audience why you are preaching to them unless you are prepared to live up to the reason. Also, never tell them what they may expect to take home with them unless you are sure that they will leave with the heart of the matter in their pockets. Still within the parameters of what you expect to say, promises may be the best use of the introductory time.

Audience Analysis

An invitation to speak to an audience puts a Christian communicator under obligation. The first preoccupying questions about the audience begin to fly. Who are they? What are their creeds, compulsions, commitments? Why do they want me to speak to them? In their excellent book, *Audiences, Messages, Speakers,*[6] John L. Vohs and G. P. Mohrman discuss three types of audience analysis: demographic analysis, motive analysis, and range-of-receptivity analysis. The three issues are all-important for the Christian communicator.

Demographics play a more important part in

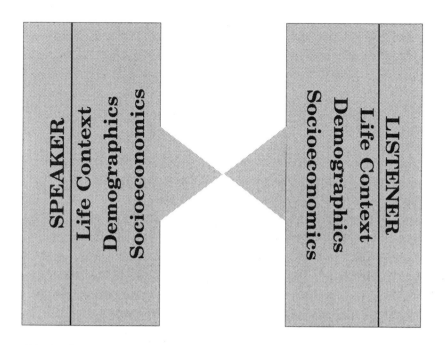

Christian receptivity than we would like to admit. Christians in different regions of America hold different convictions about what constitutes sin. Milwaukee Lutherans who work in a brewery might be more tolerant of beer drinking than Southern Baptists on tobacco plantations in Georgia. Certain Southern areas would be more politically conservative than their more permissive New England cousins.

Motives are also important. The first three minutes of a sermon often do more to measure the analysis than all of the study that is done ahead of time. Years of practice may be required to analyze with expertise. Even more time may be required to teach the Christian communicator how to adjust his or her speech in process. The final chapter of this book will be given entirely to this subject. For now it should at least be mentioned that the speech-before-the-speech will tell the preacher or speaker volumes. The audience's motives and range of receptivity are the part of the critical "first scan" of our listeners.

The final issue of audience analysis is *range of receptivity*. How do listeners receive the sermon and the various words of the sermon? Homonyms can be a real problem. I remember a radio preacher from my childhood who preached on Ezekiel 24:23 ("your tires shall be upon your head") as a prophecy of automotive rubber rationing during World War II. Home folks found his preaching well within their range of receptivity. But had the preacher been addressing a college of rabbis who knew the word translated *tire* meant "turban," the effect would have been lost.

Homonyms and near-homonyms are ever a problem in communication. I remember a young child who sang (as a line from the hymn "We're Marching to Zion"), "and thus surround the throne," as "and dust around the throne!" Donald Coggins, the archbishop of Canterbury, told of a preacher who announced to his congregation his intention of preaching on "The Blessed Paraclete." A woman in the congregation leaned over to her husband and asked, "Why would he want to devote a whole sermon to a bird?"

Audience analysis can tell us how a person will hear the word that is spoken. The words plain and plane are homonyms, and their meanings would be differently received by Native Americans and airline pilots. A gymnast and a cowpuncher would contrive two separate images of the one word horse. To a monk, an office might be a place of service; to a business man, his room for corporate management. People hear from widely differing life contexts. Their context determines how they receive what the speaker says, not what the speaker actually intended to say.

The story may be thumbworn but it is an excellent example of homonyms and communication problems.

An old farmer told the sad tale of his failing marriage to a divorce counselor.

"My wife wants a divorce."

"Does she have grounds?" asked the counselor.

"Yep! 'Bout twenty acres," answered the farmer.

"No, no, no, I mean does she have a real suit?"

"Yep, a couple of them; she wears one during the week, the 'tother on Sunday."

"No . . . I mean does she have a case?"

"Sure does. I gave her a little black case last Christmas."

Finally in sheer frustration the counselor asked forthrightly, "What seems to be the problem in your marriage?"

"Well, the woman says we just can't communicate."

The farmer and his wife apparently were on the edge of divorce over homonyms.

The audience range of receptivity will tell us whether or not real communication is occurring. Remember Alice's communication problems with the Red Queen?

Ere the Red Queen began . . . "Can you answer useful questions?" she said. "How is bread made?"

"I know that!" Alice cried eagerly. "You take some flour . . ."

"Where do you pick the flower?" the white queen asked, "In the garden or in the hedges?"

"Well, it isn't picked at all," Alice explained, "It's ground . . ."

"How many acres of ground?" asked the White

Queen. "You mustn't leave out so many things."

"Fan her head!" the Red Queen anxiously interrupted. "She'll be feverish after so much thinking."

. . . .

"She's all right again now," said the Red Queen. "Do you know languages? What is the French for fiddle-dee-dee?"

"Fiddle-dee-dee's not English," Alice replied gravely.

"Who said it was?" said the Red Queen.

Alice thought she saw a way out of the difficulty this time. "If you'll tell me what language fiddle-dee-dee is, I'll tell you the French for it!" she exclaimed triumphantly.

But the Red Queen drew herself up rather stiffly and said, "Queens never make bargains!"

"I wish queens never asked questions," Alice thought to herself.[7]

Alice discovered that queens as a class do represent a particular range of receptivity problems. Homonyms were obviously the problem between the Red Queen and Alice. But Alice learned a lot about communication in this brief exchange.

What was important to Alice is absolutely essential to preachers. The better preachers get at audience analysis, the clearer their communication.

The Speaker's Credentials

Never forget that just as the preacher is going through audience analysis, the audience is going through preacher analysis. Listeners are measuring and settling the same issues of speaker-audience rapport in reverse. They are asking questions such as, "Who is this person? Why should we listen?" The answers to these questions refer at least in part to the speaker's credentials.

How helpful is it to let listeners know your credentials for speaking? If it is done at all, how should it be done? One thing is sure: You must not show your credentials egocentrically. If the speech comes off as bragging authoritarianism, then of course it will damage rather than establish audience relationships. But the right to speak on the subject on which you are about to embark, shared in a casual way, may also serve as a kind of bonding. Sharing any kind of formal credentials (degrees, certificates, recognitions, awards) is never appropriate. Such information, if appropriate at all, should be shared by those who formally introduce you. To tell, in an offhand way, why and how your subject became a matter of interest and urgency to you certainly may be appropriate. Actually, it can serve your listeners' understanding.

I once addressed a group of storytellers by telling them a story that was not part of my formal address. This was a practical, narrative preface. It explained to them why I had chosen the subject I did. How is it that a storyteller gains the right to coach other people in the art of telling stories? My pre-sermon dealt with that very issue. It was a rather humorous tale about the second sermon I ever preached. My first sermon was a disaster, not just for the listeners but for my own self-confidence. My first attempt at preaching was precept-oriented and void of stories. My second sermon worked much better because it was based on a simple Bible story. This narrative style of my second sermon helped me extend the time-limit of my first sermon, which lasted three minutes. My first, storyless sermon left me ashamed. I felt embarrassed that I was unable to preach a real, hefty, Oklahoma, thirty-minute sermon.

This pre-sermon anecdote touched off a first-sermon reminiscence in many of the preachers who were in the audience that day. In this offhanded way I was able to establish a strong audience identity. My similarities with my hearers did not put them off with arrogance. It drew them in as fellow strugglers. Such relational credentials will often be welcomed by the listeners. If used, they should be offered informally in the four following categories.

What I've Learned

This question presumes not an academic answer, but a casual answer. Nobody wants to know what you have learned in a degree program. Everybody wants to know what you have learned by experience. The School of Hard Knocks is the only "school-larnin" your listeners generally care much about. Perhaps the only exception to this rule would have to do with those sermons and lectures given at a school you once attended. But even there you will do better when you tell of your personal experiences at the school. Celebrating your academic acquisitions even to alumni sells poorly.

What you have learned must be something that your listeners want to learn. Better yet, it should be something they need to learn. But how can we use what we have learned to help our audience? We must show what we have learned without being verbose. I remember once sharing the platform with a certain psychologist. His rambling style of preaching taught me two things: experience must be relevant, and it must be applicable. His childhood had been a disaster. He had wandered from one unhappy-abusive-soul-damaging experience to another unhappy-abusive-soul-damaging experience. He had learned many lessons through long, sad bouts with his unfeeling parents. These experiences may have been instructive to him, but he didn't evoke much audience concern about them. He tried to build a case for enticing his listeners to hear his sad tales. But, alas, we did not relate. His misery was intrinsic, and after all, we had problems of our own. Through a series of sermons, his crowd continued to dwindle. He seemed unaware that he was using the audience as his psychiatrist. They quickly guessed that his sermons were meeting only his needs, not theirs. His learning experiences did not strike a relational interest in those who heard him.

How can we use our own pilgrimage to illustrate what we have learned? How can we break our large experiences into bite-sized applications? We must keep interrupting our own saga (especially if we sense interest is flagging) and tell the audience what this learning experience once meant to us. Then we can tell them what it now means to them. At such junctures we will also be reinforcing in them the key bonding issue, "Here's how I'm like you!"

How Long I Took to Learn It

Do we have to take much space telling them how long we spent learning those lessons? Certainly not! What is important is that such lessons find strong applications. Here may be a great place for autobiography. Illustrating the faults and foibles of our learning process will often hold humor. Maximize your pilgrimage at this point.

A case in point may be Tony Campolo's "My God Is a Party Animal" (a vintage Campolo sermon titled in various other ways). This sermon has biblical exposition, personal value change, and a great deal of humor. In his account, Campolo tells us how long it took him to learn his lesson. In this very famous story, Tony meets a flock of warm-hearted prostitutes who had served up a lot of "love" but had never experienced much of it. The illustrating of his involvement took him some days to learn. But his practical relating of his experience is delightful and profound. Best of all, his lesson is given little by little. He narrates as he instructs. Similarly, your audience should feel enthralled and feel your experiences most useful.

Ways I've Found It to Be True

How, at this point, do we offer the application? The best application is done as the truth of our experiences is reinforced. Again, it should all be done inductively. Describing what we have learned teaches others without using high-pressure salesmanship. We offer narrative information but do not compel them to apply it in any particular way. They remain in charge of how they will use our experience. Our experience simply relates to their minds and calls for gentle endorsement. This induction testimonial leads them very easily to the reason we offered them our experience. It is up to them to take the fourth and final step.

How You Can Learn It Faster

This part of power communication assumes that, while experience may be the best teacher, it is rarely the fastest. The best part of our motivation lies in the

What I've Learned

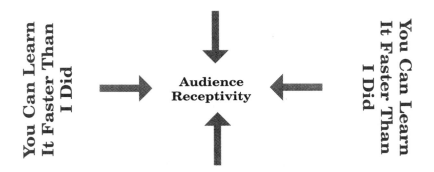

The Ways I've Found My Lessons to Be True

thorough description of our experience. This leads our hearer to say within, "Aha, I can take a short cut and spare myself the speaker's agony."

Remember now, we are talking about how we warm up to an audience. We are not speaking about how we disseminate our content. We are really talking about the information that we give an audience up front to induce them to give us their attention. It might be argued that we, in this testimonial experience, are giving them too much up front. Will we not be giving the meat of the discussion rather than merely establishing the relationship out of which we shall later relate to them?

Again, I stress that I am not talking about giving them the main content of the sermon. I am talking about giving them enough of ourselves and our learning experiences to get them to listen. Later in the body of our argument, we may want to give them still more of ourselves. Our pilgrimage will usually be welcome.

What we have learned from life may need to be upfront in our sermons, the pre-sermon out as a bridge to the audience. This initial bridging will let them see that we are practically experienced in the school of trial and error.

It must be obvious that this pre-sermon confession is a brief one. In fact, the words *sermon brief* may be the best way to catalog what we are saying. In no way is it a give-away of all that is to come; it is instead an incitement to interest. Lee Iacocca opened his autobiography with an incantation of curses against Henry Ford III. Ford had fired him after years of company loyalty. Iacocca bore a terse grudge. His brief incantation told the reader what his Ford Motor experiences had cost him. It was pre-argument, but his brief incantation prepared the reader to hear. It moves the reader up to chapter 1 with an eagerness that said, "I too have known betrayal in my life and will again. I can't wait to read this book." This preface took very little space in the book, but the author used it well to develop instant rapport.

Making Friends

In the initial moments of building a listener relationship, the key has more to do with feeling than argument. Arguments are not heard until the emotive sense of speakers and listeners have merged. After we have reached an involved and relational oneness, there will come a time for reaching a togetherness in our argument.

Let us conclude this chapter with an example of this first key. A beloved pastor of tenure may have so warmed his people over the years that Sunday brings them into church always ready to hear. A bridge of communication between pastor and congregation has been built by a longstanding relationship. The congregation is always ready to hear the sermon. Because a life has been well used, sermonic expectancy is as high as it will ever go. Any guest speaker who moves into this environment will be tried for authenticity and rapport against a very high, congregational standard.

Finding common ground for communication is difficult; it must be done one audience at a time. All who preach face this perilous and difficult task of making friends. All who preach have chosen this high, demanding calling. And those who truly care about the needs of those they meet *en masse* must cherish this key to communicate. An unrelational approach always bolts the doors of the mind. Making friends is the key that unlocks that door.

Key Two:

Stepping Over the Ego Barrier

Give me that man that is not

passion's slave and I will

wear him in my heart's core

ay, in my heart of heart, as

I do thee.[8]

The Audience Challenge
of
Key Two

Dear Speaker:

Your ego has become a wall between yourself and me. You're not really concerned about me, are you? You're mostly concerned about whether or not this speech is really working . . . about whether or not you're doing a good job. You're really afraid that I will not applaud, aren't you? You're afraid that I won't laugh at your jokes or cry over your emotional anecdotes. You are so caught up in the issue of how I am going to receive your speech, you haven't thought much about me at all. I might have loved you, but you are so caught up in self-love that mine is really unnecessary. If I don't give you my attention its because I feel so unnecessary here.

When I see you at the microphone, I see Narcissus at his mirror. . . . Is your tie straight? Is your hair straight? Is your deportment impeccable? Is your phraseology perfect?

You seem in control of everything but your audience. You see everything so well, but us. But this blindness to us, I'm afraid, has made us deaf to you. We must go now. Sorry. Call us sometime later. We'll come back to you . . . some time in the future, when your vision is better . . . when you're real enough to see us . . . after your dreams have been shattered . . . after your heart has been broken . . . after your arrogance has reckoned with despair. Then there will be room for us in your world. Then you won't care if we applaud your brilliance. You'll be one of us.

Then you will tear down the ego wall and use those very stones to build a bridge of warm relationship. We'll meet you on that bridge. We'll hear you then. All speakers are joyously understood when they reach with understanding.

—Your Audience

The three greatest forces determining what people buy are emotional security, reassurance of worth, and ego-gratification.9 Audiences will buy what the preacher is selling only if they feel they are unfulfilled without it. This truth introduces a strong conflict between preacher and listener. The preacher has the same ego-needs as hearers. Like them, the preacher is always tempted to put his or her own needs first. So, it is never easy to set our own ego needs aside until theirs have been met. Still, this is precisely what must be done for real communication to proceed.

The

Barrier

Nan Kilkeary reminds us that the need of the communicator and communicatee can rarely be served at the same time. "Our ego keeps us from recognizing something very important about communicating . . . the other person is always more interested in themselves and what our message means to them" than they are in us.[10] The war between the preacher's ego and the listener's ego is communication's largest barrier. How speakers handle their egos facilitates or confounds understanding. The problem is easily seen when we reduce the communication setting to two. We must take speaking out of its mass setting and examine it as a conversation for two. Consider a guest speaker, whom we shall call Jim. Then shrink his whole audience to a single respondent, named John.

The Communicator's Conversation

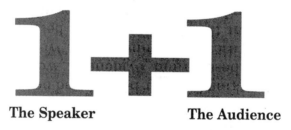

The Speaker   The Audience

Reducing the Audience to One

The wideness of audience relationship, our concern in the last chapter, is now set at two. As these friends sit talking, person to person, Jim has an agenda for John. John is likely to consider Jim's proposition only if he feels that Jim is not trying to use him for personal advantage. Relationship becomes possible only when John trusts Jim's agenda.

The egotistic agenda of many preachers has resulted in a widening contempt for church altar calls. There exists a growing feeling that evangelists must have the people "come forward" to create great publicity folders and wide reputation. Such needs tend to make synonyms of the words *God* and *Ego*. Preachers must, however, successfully convince audiences that they are in business for God, and such speakers find their sessions crowded. But those whose egos are squarely in the way do not.

Jim makes John listen, saying by his deportment, "God is my employer, and I'm in business for you." Oratorical content and speaker-esteem should team up to serve others. The audience then will give the preacher the right to be heard. Considering the importance of this gift, let us examine the greatest step a preacher can take toward the audience: the step over the ego barrier. Neal Armstrong's moon motto may serve all communicators: The step over ego should be one little step for the preacher and one giant step for the audience. Our big step toward them invites their little step toward us. Their step is psychological endorsement.

Receiving Power from Your Audience

Speaking on Their Behalf

As we established in the Introduction, communicative power is granted to the preacher, not wrested from the listeners. Arndt Halvorson reminds us that "our preaching authority stems from . . . a gift conferred by grace."[11] Two primary conditions must be met in listeners before they will grant such clout to the speaker. The first of these conditions is that the audience must feel that this presentation is really for them. There is a universal skepticism of altruism. There exists a near-universal acceptance of the adage,

"There ain't no free lunch." But in spite of this skepticism, most people come to the sermon in search of help. On the other hand, they never come anxious to gild the preacher's reputation.

In addition to this, the communiqué must be set forth in genuine ways. "Have I got a deal for you!" will always cock eyebrows. "Let me bless you!" will load the hearer's mental chamber with buckshot. The high insinuation that you want to do something papally glorious for them is the kiss of disinterest. With any real live human audience, being yourself is the place to start. As they see it, humanness defines your agenda in terms of their well-being.

Just what does being ourselves have to do with real communication? David Evans, the C.E.O. of a major restaurant franchise says, "One of the things I made up my mind to do many years ago when I first started giving speeches was to be myself, whatever that is."[12] Evans admits that we may find ambiguities about ourselves. Even so, sermon power derives not from our self-definition so much as from our self-authenticity. In other words, being what we are is even more important than knowing who we are.

Lapita Armendariz applies this principle to communication. "It's very important that I am honest about who I am, so that I can make genuine contact with the audience."[13] Until the issue of our humanity is self-proclaiming, our egos remain barriers between us and our audience. Human beings cannot hear words issued by aliens to their race. Only when the speaker is "one of us" are his or her words important to us.

A few simple rules define our humanness. First, we can't appear too eager to force our agenda on people. In strong one-on-one relationships, we can't be pushy. Second, we don't start meaningful conversations by

The Three Sides
of the
Communicator's Humility

**Talk Too Much
About Yourself**

telling people who we are, but by asking who they are. While speaking to a large audience, and since we can't ask them individually who they are, we can refrain from bragging about ourselves.

Burying Your Lead

Any bid for selfish gain in the communiqué will leave the speaker "dead in the water." The safest way to ensure that this does not happen is to refrain from being too upfront with any personal agenda.

Is this really possible? In many cases, it is not. When Bill Clinton was first elected President, he began working on his programs to eradicate the deficit. He worked on this agenda in much the same way that he campaigned. He flew to remote areas of the United States and made speeches, lobbying for support for his policies. When he made a speech, people were generally aware of why he had come. Nonetheless, he almost never launched directly into the subject matter. He was going to ask them to make major sacrifices to bail the country out of its debts. In a real sense he wanted to appear to be doing something for the nation. His national agenda was packaged in a very personal approach.

Is indirectly confronting the issue that occasions the speech not an attempt to sidestep the issue? No,

Burying the Lead

Referencing the Occasion	The Speech Before the Speech	Happy to Be Here
•••		
Address to Specific Guest	•••	•••
	Humor	Civic Compliment
•••	•••	
Relational References	Audience Thank Yous	•••
		Anecdote

Purpose of the Speech

it is rather a matter of gentle technique. Speechwriter Steven Provost says, "Often in the beginning of a speech, I bury the lead. I put the central point I want to make not right at the beginning but two or three minutes into the speech. I subscribe to the ninety-second theory. You have ninety-seconds to gain their attention . . . by burying the lead, you raise the opportunity to get attention in a variety of ways."[14]

The buried lead is an attempt to build rapport without directly confronting the subject. It is a mark of sensibility. Any attempt to get the listeners to move too directly to your agenda may antagonize them. It may put them on the defensive so much that they will be unable to hear your presentation. A direct beginning may set audience prejudices firmly against you and your message.

In beginning an address that will ask much of the listener, humor is one of the most effective ways to begin. Daniel O'Keefe writes: "Where positive effects of humor are found, they tend to most directly involve enhancement of the audience's liking for the communicator—and thus occasionally the trustworthiness of the communicator. Small amounts of appropriate humor thus may have small enhancing effects on perceived trustworthiness, but are unlikely to affect assessments of the communicator's competence."[15]

An audience that laughs together will find it easier to relate when the sermon becomes demanding. I remember an occasion when the music committee of our church wanted to buy a new organ. After much study, they had decided that the kind of organ they wanted to buy was a Rodgers organ. They had opted against a similar bid from Allen Organs in making this decision. Because the chairman of the trustees liked the price of the Allen organ better, he became convinced that the church should buy that brand. Although he knew nothing about music in general, or organs in particular, he became dead set on the issue. As he locked his mind on buying the Allen organ, the music committee dug in their heels for purchasing the Rodgers. The conflict solidified into a congregational Armageddon. The music committee saw the obstinate trustee as old six-sixty-six. It seemed, at last, that tension could go no further. Bloodshed was imminent.

So I quit moderating and began refereeing. I opted for us to laugh rather than fight our way out of deadlock. "Look," I said, "I think we ought to honor the music committee and buy a Rodgers organ for three reasons: First of all, Rodgers organs are built by Roy and Dale [Roy Rogers was a popular cowboy of the day]; second, they are great for singing "Happy Trails to You" [Roy and Dale's theme song]; and third, they have an electronic stop that whinnies [like Roy's horse, Trigger]." Laughter erupted, erasing the tension. We were then free to go on asking the people to make a free choice. Having laughed together they found it easy to sacrifice together.

Four Evidences You Have Broken the Ego Barrier

There are four evidences to consider when crossing the ego barrier. These evidences have nothing to do with helping the audience know if you have broken it. If you do it well, as far as the audience is concerned, you will never have established an ego barrier. As we are in the process of delivering our sermon, interest (theirs, not ours) will tell us if we have transcended the barrier. In short, people do not listen to any information coming to them from across the ego barrier.

It is interesting that, although people will hear nothing across the barrier, they will *send* messages across it. They will sometimes "grin" their antipathies across the barrier. They will "harpoon" them across. They will certainly "sneer" them across. In the days of vaudeville, people threw vegetables across that barrier. Such "splats" rarely stop a contemporary sermon. Nonetheless, a volley of nonverbal messages do sail across it. Darts of insolence are all fired by hostile eyes. Javelins of stubborn resolve are thrown across it. Steam, nearly visible, issues from the ears of hot audiences. Such body language is nonverbal communication of the highest order. This ugly feedback will tell you that you have established a firm barrier. More gentle indicators will tell you there are no barriers in communication process. Let's look at four such indicators, one at a time.

Demonstrating Apparent Ease

Audience tension and the preacher's self-centeredness keep the same company. Most of the time when we become unmanageably tense in front of a crowd, it is because we have too many of our own interests at stake. Notice, I said "unmanageably." Any time we speak, there should be a reasonable amount of tension. This tension comes from a natural nervousness that we acquire because of our fear of public speaking. But when too much of our own agenda is riding on any address, we may find that our motivational goals subvert our wise control. Passion, overcharged, goes wild.

Learning to cope with a natural amount of nervousness is a part of the communicator's discipline. As W. F. Strong reminds us, "Speech anxiety never goes away no matter how much experience you have. However . . . you learn to manage it. Through exposure to anxiety you inoculate yourself against its extreme effects."[16]

The word *extreme* is the issue here. Each new speaking opportunity should go on presenting the speaker with that healthy tension that causes us to struggle with the need to do our best. But it should not debilitate us with that cold, counterproductive terror.

Extreme nervousness may cause the audience to read us as totally egocentric. This is a natural indictment. Hearers ask themselves if we would be so concerned if we were preaching on *their* behalf. A young defense lawyer at his first trial may quit thinking about what his client has at stake in a trial. He may be absorbed in winning the case because it's important to his career. When the lawyer's need to win outpaces his concern for the client, his nervousness may get out of hand.

In a more directly applicable way, let us examine the preacher's ego. What is the "money" on the sermon? Every communicator's psyche is constructed from some drive for self-approval. We all have a terrible need to succeed in front of others. We all want those complimentary strokes we get by speaking well. This universal need to succeed can drive us to forget our audience. Avoid the egotism as your audience will avoid you. Don't forget, they also have their needs. Our communiqué must serve them first. But there are those special times in the life of any preacher (like those of the attorney mentioned above) when the "money on the game" will be critical to the speaker's reputation. For instance, a first sermon in a new parish is vital. So is candidating sermon before a search committee. These sermons can cause ego to rise to stifling levels of self-concern. Our communications skills may suffer and the audience will quickly sense that this sermon is being preached for some other reason than their benefit.

Demonstrating Humility

Pride always obscures the message and usually the messenger as well. "Pride goeth before destruction" (Prov. 16:18); it also hides great truths behind "wideload" self-importance. Humility is not a state to be struggled for and achieved; it is a naturalness that occurs when you achieve spiritual perspective. Humility does not intentionally diminish who you are. It does not come about by gritting the teeth and saying, "Oh, to be nothing!"

Rather, platform humility is a twofold process. The first step is to keep your task more central in your own

Two Ego States of Preachers

The Non-Communicative
Sermon

The Communicative
Sermon

eyes than you yourself are. A simple word of caution: Never let your message so occupy your thought that you lose awareness of your mystique. This may be oversimplifying, but no message, however gripping its hold on the speaker, will suffice to distract the audiences from a "slip that shows" or (heaven forbid!) a gaping fly. But there is too little room in any preacher to be both full of a message and full of the self.

Humility is more than being lost in the grip of one's subject. Humility also has a spiritual ring about it. John Oman once said, "Unless the pulpit is the place where you are the humblest in giving God's message, it is certain to be the place where you are vainest in giving your own."[17]

But in preaching as in developing the inner life, humility is not so much diminishing our self-importance as simply standing next to Jesus. It is not possible for any communicator to have a dynamic walk with Christ without seeing His all-surpassing greatness. This towering Jesus, by sheer contrast, will always displace our self-importance. When there is a natural hunger for union with Christ, the entire issue of humility is automatically achieved. Evangelists are complimented so often that they have a hard time building this humility. Be sure that your subject matter is more important to you than you are.

A fine line separates affirmation from criticism. We want people to affirm what we say; however, too much affirmation breeds arrogance. It builds the ego barrier. But as too much affirmation spoils the communiqué, so does a continual diet of criticism. How difficult it is to see our real worth when we have been drubbed to the stake of audience contempt. Whipped by such rebuke, the self grows vacant. Our lost confidence erodes our self-esteem and devours the passion of our delivery.

Demonstrating Transparency

Transparency is that wonderful see-through state of being. Opaque glass hides what is beyond it. What is hidden makes us afraid or skeptical. Illusionists grow wealthy by hiding the way they alter our perception of reality. They make us believe a lie, which they alone can varnish with illusion. We cannot see through their contrivances. While we may be wooed with their illusions, we do know that they are not real. We know they hide the real from us in their cloaks or hats or magic chests, and we are enchanted by their trickery.

Deep down, audiences are resentful of most truths made so obscure they cheat our senses. Edward Markquart said, "People want their preachers to be authentic human beings . . . who experience all the same feelings and struggles as the laity, who do not hide behind the role of Reverend 'so and so.'"[18] Illusion and trickery are the deceptive trade of mind-benders.

Truth and discovery, however, are the products of openness. Confessional preachers gain the confidence of an audience. Transparency is an automatic indicator to yourself that you have shattered the ego barrier. Why? Because the only way we achieve such transparency is by running the risk of self-revelation. Transparency always involves some confessional preaching. It occurs when we lay open the weaker portions of our lives. Confession builds a three-way relationship between our audience, our subject matter, and ourselves.

Such openness may involve more emotional looseness than we would prefer to unveil in the lectern or pulpit. Often we become most transparent by the loss of self-control in front of others. Some of the most impassioned and listenable sermons I have ever heard were those where the preacher parted with composure. By willingly becoming less intelligible, they became more believable.

But emotional exposés do have their limitations. The first time that the national evangelist, Jimmy Swaggart, lost emotional control and confessed his sin, many were moved. But successive tearful confessions did not improve his credibility. Transparency has value only if the confessor has a high level of moral values. The coupling of such openness to goodness anchors the soul of the speaker in a sea of warm identity.

Transparency, like humility, is not so much a goal one achieves as a virtue one possesses. Those who have transparency are fortunate indeed. They can talk about themselves in a natural and unassuming way. Those without transparency feel very uncomfortable speaking confessionally. It is all but impossible for them to be transparent. Do those without transparency have any hope of acquiring the quality?

The use of compelling personal illustrations can be of great help here. My logic flies in the face of such homiletical giants as David Buttrick. He cautions us against using personal illustrations. But I want to take a stand in favor of them. Self-disclosure is an authentic way to arrive at audience identity. They permit a critical transparency that makes the speaker believable.

A caution should be sounded: personal illustrations are easier to come by than is the discipline of sound study. Speakers who are good at telling stories can actually turn off their audience. They can be guilty of talking about themselves at the expense of good Bible study and content oratory. Speakers who use too many personal anecdotes do not eliminate the ego barrier. They raise it even higher.

I recently shared a program with a self-centered preacher whose long, strung-together, personal anecdotes pronounced him the most arrogant of souls. He bludgeoned the audience with tales of his codependent and dysfunctional family life until we were weary. The worst that might be said of him was that he seemed to have little awareness of his egoism. He seemed not to know he was self-centered. He thought his lectures were serving others. Such levels of self-centeredness are so psychologically entrenched they are nearly impossible to heal.

Demonstrating the Ability to Laugh at Yourself

Transparency and the ability to laugh at ourselves are values so closely related that it is hard to separate them. People who can laugh at their mistakes—even as they are making them—are delightfully transparent. But arriving at this level of transparency is hard for two reasons. First, preaching is normally very serious work. When we get our tongues twisted up in pulpit bloopers, we feel ashamed that we have injured the deep spiritual truths we wanted to convey. Still, a blooper is a blooper. Yet we were so intent on being both serious and spiritual, we often feel hot shame at our errant delivery. But it does invite laughter. It may be hard to ditch our high preachment and deal with our humorous *faux pas*. It gets very hard to laugh at such times. Still, if we get red in the face and become flustered at our idiocy, we show that we are taking ourselves too seriously.

What happens when an audience senses that we are embarrassed over our mistake? They probably sense that we thought we were incapable of making a mistake. The flustered mystique probably says we were so centered on our platform "godhood" that we were embarrassed to admit our mortality.

A friend of mine during my seminary days preached a wonderful and very serious sermon from Genesis about Lot "pitching his tent toward Sodom." Instead of saying "Lot pitched his tent," he actually said that Lot "pinched his . . ." (well, never mind). The point is that in his very serious sermon on sin and repentance, he sensed by the broad smiles afflicting every face that he had committed an unmentionable pulpit blooper. He stopped his sermon and asked out loud, "Folks, did I say what I think I said?" The question was all it took to free the audience up for howls of laughter. Fortunately, in spite of his redness, my friend was able to join in. The seriousness was lost. In fact, the whole sermon was shot, but humor owned the day. Really, humanity owned the day. Best of all, a young prophet had demonstrated enough transparency to guarantee him a long tenure in the same pulpit.

"To err is human," affirms the proverb. To laugh at ourselves and err publicly is especially human. All audiences delight at catching the pious at their

FOUR EVIDENCES OF
THE SPEAKER'S TRANSPARENCY

1. Confessional Preaching

2. A Comfortable Demeanor

3. The Balanced Use of Personal Illustrations

4. An Ability to Laugh at Ourselves

humanity. Welcome, therefore, all occasions of such joy. Your occasional idiocy may afford you a gathering of friends. Stand with them for your own soul's mockery. Life will reward you with trust.

The Grand Evidences That You Are Speaking on Their Behalf

There are two grand evidences by which we can tell if we are speaking for their benefit and not our own. In considering these grand evidences, we are dealing with the priorities of communication. We have already dealt with that thin line that exists between what is good for us and what is good for them. When we are speaking to benefit our own career and community image, we are not in business for them. An audience will sense this instantly. I forever remind myself of two adages. I've already mentioned the first: There ain't no free lunch! This proverb will be in the audience's mind as we speak. All the time that we are presenting what we think will be a good deal for them, they will be asking themselves, "Why is the speaker so interested in my welfare? Why is he or she working so hard to give me such a good deal?"

Because this will be a primary question in their minds, we must not thickly lay any obvious generosity on them. Be reasonable, not slick, in telling them how good your good deal really is. I always flinch when I pick up the telephone and am greeted by a telemarketer. I know when he starts telling me all that I have just won (and the gifts in these latter, slick times have become most impressive) that he's really working on his own commission. I know he wants to soak himself in the lush benefits of his own lingo while he strips me of cash. The slicker his presentation, the more wary I become. Why? Because my life, so far, has never been greatly advanced by phone calls from strangers completely fascinated by my welfare.

I once sat through a high-pressure real estate spiel. The saleswoman was there to clue me in on the best deal of my life. She wanted to "help" me as I prepared for my retirement years. To consider the wonderful things she was going to do for me, she had lured me to the heart of the Rockies. In her office she plopped me down in front of a huge glass panel. Framed in the heart of the Wolf Creek Pass mountains, she made me drool about actually owning my own piece of Colorado. She had a sparkle in her eye, and she was gorgeous; it was all like buying a piece of land from Julia Roberts. She had lured me to her "seductive" lecture by giving me four free days in a wonderful condominium. I ate scrumptious meals from Belshazzar's buffet. She had even given me a one-hundred-dollar bill the first moment that we met so I could really enjoy touring through my "new mountain home." Of course, this home had not even been built. In fact, I was shortly to discover (right *after* I bought the lot) that there weren't even any roads built to my lot. I would have to shimmy down the mountainside just to get to my lot. This was a detail that "Julia" forgot to mention. She also forgot to mention that the plot had not been surveyed, so there was no electric service to my beautiful unbuilt home. I still, however, would be charged a monthly electric bill, and, of course, a country club fee, even though the actual country club and golf course were not there either. Yet she assured us that she only existed to help us "plan our golden years." "Did we have a little gold that we could put down on our dream, right now?" We were mad with joy! We gave her a large part of our life savings. It was the least we could do—after all she had done for us. In the next five years, we lost all the gold we had given her, and our golden dreams went down the tubes. How could it happen? She appeared so gorgeous, saintly, and altruistic. She seemed to epitomize that splendid blend of Mother Teresa and Marilyn Monroe.

I went to a revival meeting once where an evangelist tried to convince me that God would repay me fourfold if I would just support his ministry. But having looked at real estate in Colorado, I was absorbed in doubt. The general rule in either sermonizing or selling real estate is this: The slicker your spiel, the less credible you appear. "There ain't no free lunch!"

A second proverb belongs to the speaker alone. It will come to mind quite frequently as we speak. It is this: Is there really any such thing as altruism? I must confess that no matter how much I exalt my own selflessness as I preach, I continually ask myself, "Supposing they do all that I am asking in this sermon? What's in it for me?" I have never asked myself that without receiving a whole host of replies. First of all, one of the things that's nearly always in it for me is an honorarium. Would I even be there speaking to them if I thought they might not pay me? Second, if they do all that I say, won't that look good for my career goals? Won't the word get around about how brilliantly I've done? As the questions roll in, I realize (when I am totally honest) that the better the audience responds to my propositions the more my own wealth and status grow.

When I am honest, I know that I am rarely there on behalf of the audience alone. If I try to tell them that, I do introduce the possibility of a real credibility loss. Preachers appear to be saying, "It's because I love Christ so much that He has enabled me to be totally selfless." All such talk should be passe in the modern

TWO AUDIENCE ADAGES
OF SKEPTICISM

1. THERE AIN'T NO FREE LUNCH

So how much
will all this cost
me, Buster?

2. THERE'S NO SUCH THING AS ALTRUISM

So what's in this
for you, Buster?

sermon. Hearers will better believe us if we devote ourselves to helping them understand our sermons. This means that at all costs we must avoid a rhetoric of selfish power.

It seems to me that there are only two kinds of rhetoric as we think about breaking the ego barrier:

- The rhetoric of selfish power, selfishly used and selfishly applied;
- The rhetoric of servanthood.

Breaking the ego barrier requires this rhetoric of servanthood. But achieving servanthood sermons is only possible when we submit ourselves to God. But if our hearers are ever to believe that we exist primarily for them, we must learn to keep their interest.

Avoiding the Rhetoric of Selfish Power

In speakers, there is a rhetoric that keeps company with a lust for power. It usually has a ramrod tone about it. That tone is easily picked up by the audience. It is so subtly pervasive, however, that it is not always easily discovered by the speaker. A general rule for knowing whether it has crept into our oratorical style is to ask ourselves this question: *Am I still preaching and teaching in the inductive mode?* Remember that induction calls for the speaker to present information while the audience negotiates the process of analyzing, assimilating, and accepting the truth.[19]

If this were the only reason to communicate inductively, it would be a strong one. Induction lays the onus for responding to a speech at the feet of the hearers. Induction offers counsel. It does not try to force a conclusion. It is not possible in the inductive mode for the speaker to grab for power. Induction consciously puts the "grab" in the audience's hands. In the inductive mode, power is a matter of the speaker's incarnational surrender to the hearer. This surrender lies at the heart of the servant sermon. There are three evidences that we are avoiding rhetoric of power as we preach.

Evidence #1: Inductive speaking. We know we are avoiding the rhetoric of selfish power when we are inductive in our discourse. Harsh imperative phrases will drop out. An informative, counseling style will be born. *You must* or *you should* will become infrequent. The chief pronouns will usually shift from *you* to *we*. As the *mustiness, shouldiness,* and *shaltiness* fade from our communiqué, attention grows. Inductive speaking allows oratory to become what it was always intended to be, a word of counsel: "Come now, and let us reason together" (Isa. 1:18). The prophet's counsel is the basis for our counseling style.

A word that goes with induction is *indicative*. In the indicative mood, we give out information without demanding anything of the hearer. The customary stance in sermons of fifty years ago was to preach in the imperative mood. If we were to phrase modern communiqués in terms of that old imperative sermonic tone, we might still be saying things like "Turn or burn!" But if we put this in the indicative style, we would say, "Repentance could be a very vital idea to you. In fact it could be the single most important issue of a lifetime. Examine it, and make up your mind about it. Please keep in mind that, while you decide what the Bible says, there is but one alternative to repentance. You will, of course, need to make up your mind about that too."

If it is objected that it takes more time to deal inductively with issues, all that can be said is yes. But only induction leaves the listener in charge. Modern congregations will not listen to sermons that strip away their right to remain in charge of their destiny. So, induction is not just a way to avoid the rhetoric of self: it is the *only* way to get hearers involved. Again, all *shouldy*, *shalty*, and *oughty* talk must invite open counsel from which the hearers decide.

Evidence #2: Natural speaking. A second evidence showing that we are avoiding the rhetoric of power is to be sure that we are speaking naturally. We are to speak as if we were in a one-on-one conversation. Our words, delivered conversationally, will never stray too close to ostentation. A rhetoric of power always borrows executive image and uses swelling tones to push its agenda. Before large crowds there is always a tendency to turn from saying things in a natural way. We then push forward, feeling that, in ourselves, we are somehow not impressive enough to hold attention. Such feelings derive from insecurity. They believe the truth that our own words are the only thing that we *can* use. Our uninflated words are naturally us. They allow our own personality to communicate. Phillips Brooks in another century gave us preaching's most basic definition: "truth through personality." This definition holds for all communicative forms.

The Persuader's Pronouns

Inductive	Executive
WE	YOU
Indicative	Imperative

The Conversational Approach	The Oratorical Demand

The Question	couldn't we can't we may we	The Command	you must you should you have to
Reason	one on one conversation	Ultimatum	chain of command suggestion

Evidence #3: Journalistic speaking. In addition to using our own words, there is a third and final evidence of servant communication.

We develop a journalistic style, assuring us that we have steered clear of a rhetoric of power. This skill can be honed by watching a network anchorperson. Newscasters customarily use the briefest means possible to communicate powerfully and simply. Remember that simplicity not only sells, it is the key to avoiding ostentation. A journalistic style majors on getting out the facts. The two parts of speech that do this best are nouns and verbs. Haddon Robinson says, "Verbs like nouns wake up the imagination when they are precise. He 'went' gets him there but not as clearly as 'crawled,' 'stumbled,' 'shuffled,' 'lurched.' She 'shouts,' 'shrieks,' 'rants,' 'whispers,' tells us what 'says' does not."[20]

I myself call this process *synonym sifting*. This process of synonym sifting finds the strongest possible words to make the most descriptive statement. The key is to use strong words without becoming ostentatious. Adjectives tempt us to ostentation. Needless to say, adjectives are also the key to description. We must not neglect descriptive language. We must, however, remember that adjectives can over-ornament our nouns. Heavily decorated nouns over-ornament our self-opinion. Their grandeur keeps us from seeing ourselves in ordinary ways. Nouns and verbs are basic in common parlance. Adjectives may mark us as a people of excess. Use adjectives but control them, lest they lure you away from a crisp journalistic style. Above all, never let adjectives infatuate you.

Working Developmentally to Keep Their Interest

There are five aspects to a developmental approach in holding audience interest. All five demonstrate the preacher's willingness to start where the listeners are. Beginning with the hearers is the first step in bridging the communication gap.

I once asked a friend if he would like to attend our Easter services with me. "I wouldn't even know where to get the tickets," he demurred. His answer reminded me of the understanding gap between church attenders and non-church attenders. A rhetoric of power wraps its speech in the horrible assumption that everybody's understanding is mine. Such a view is always naïve; it is often an assumption born in the preacher's arrogance. As long as any sermon proceeds from naïveté or arrogance, very little communication can occur.

Our willingness to begin where others are shows that we are free of a need to control others. It further says we are possessed of a need to understand them. Sad is the communicator who is unwilling to begin on this elementary level. He is in effect shouting, like a brusque father to a dawdling child, "Hurry up . . . now!" Sensitive preachers take nothing for granted. They are counseling communicators. They are content to be sure that they have slowed down to walk at the child's pace.

The first of these five developmental steps is this: *Start your communication simply.* This means that you are willing to deliver your speech at a rate the audience can understand. It also means you are moving the content at a rate with which they can keep pace. You are always moving from a slow rate of rhetoric to a more challenging pace. This occurs with intelligibility only if you pause here and there during the early part of your sermon. Each time you stop, you must carefully correlate the various parts of your unfolding argument. You must be willing to move in this slow, defined fashion. If not, you are more interested in your agenda for your sermon than theirs; you have shifted from a rhetoric of concord to a rhetoric of power.

A second element of development is this: *Develop your sermon from a less positive to a more positive rhetoric.* Employing this principle says that you are interested in ending positively. Brent Filson said it well: "A sure way to kill a good sermon is to end pessimistically: You can have a pessimistic conclusion to an essay, a novel, a movie, or a newspaper editorial, but never, never to a speech."[21] All ideas necessary to a positive communiqué should be presented in their entirety. The direction of sermonic flow should always move from less likable to more likable themes.

But what does such positivism have to do with avoiding a rhetoric of power? Audience-centered preachers care about their audiences. They want people to feel good when the sermon is over. Non-servant sermons consistently slog listeners in pessimism. Not all good sermons can end buoyantly, but a consistent diet of negative endings will cause hearers to abandon us.

Still, good communicators are more than cheerleaders. They are charged with the heavy responsibility of always making others feel good. In fact, when our work is done well, our best sermons create a sense of spiritual need in the hearers. Such need causes them to feel bad about their inadequacies. But preachers who really care about others avoid a rhetoric that dismisses the audience's pain as trivial.

Such preachers demonstrate that they are interested in servanthood. Joy is to be the character of the servant of Christ. Joy is to be characteristic of the sermon as well.

Let us consider a third element of development in a sermon which demonstrates that we are interested in stepping over the ego barrier. The third element is this: *Move within your sermon from looser to tighter informational structures.* What about this movement indicates a rhetoric of counsel? The focus in such a developmental move says that you are not interested in just dumping your information on the audience and running out of the room. As the audience begins to move with you, you can tighten the sermon's focus. Gradually you can accelerate the speed of the information as your hearers bless your presentation with generous doses of interest.

In speaking to a great many college assemblies, I have discovered that most students are very diverse in maturity and interest. The most intellectually mature of these are ready to hear everything I have to say. Those who are fledgling in their maturity need me to be gentle in the pace of my delivery. To those who want me to move faster, I may appear to be dawdling. If I use humor to retard the pace, I may appear to be "horsing around." Still, to those who are struggling to keep up, my casual delivery *does* make sense. To them my pace is keeping faith with their comprehension.

This approach is what baby-boomer pastors call a user-friendly style. I don't object to the term. This is a day when it is dangerous to presume that our audiences know more than they actually do. But I warn all of those who push the user-friendly methodology. We should indeed be user-friendly; but to start "lite" and stay "lite" will not serve all our hearers very well. In fact, it may negate our obligation to inform our hearers. The sermon is God's document first and the people's document next. In a rhetoric of servant-hood the sermon never belongs solely to the commu-nicator. No selfish use should be made of it.

A fourth developmental step that shows our concern for the hearer is this: *Supply all the information they need.* Remember that good communication calls order out of chaos. Conversely, forgetting key information leads to confusion. It takes time to build an orderly argument, and our willingness to move slowly is our gift to the listener. But do we fail to preach content messages merely because we want to be kind to the spiritually uninformed? If so, we may commit the sin of empty entertainment. John MacArthur warns us away from sterile eloquence: "What value is . . . the eloquence of Apollos if you have nothing worthwhile to say? You cannot make up in zeal what you lack in sub-stance."[22]

This fifth step of the development of the sermon is this: *Move from emotional ease to emotional intensi-ty.* Step five is similar to step three. In the third step we move from loose to tight structures of presenta-tion. In this step we are interested in being sure that we never get too intense in our own emotional involvement. Emotional intensity scares people. They sometimes feel as though they are hearing a weirdo or fanatic. Yet, it is not always possible, if we are preaching a key sermon, to be low key. In fact, passion is as important as caution in preaching.

Passion is a must. Any communication without some intensity will be flat and unappealing. But let it be said here that speakers with Gatling-gun zeal may scare or bore with their hyper-tense delivery. Such emotional delivery may cause a reaction from the audience which actually inhibits persuasion.[23]

The Five Aspects
of Developmental Interest

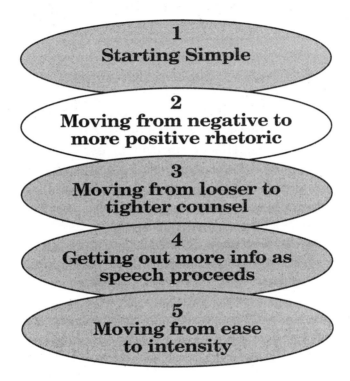

1
Starting Simple

2
Moving from negative to
more positive rhetoric

3
Moving from looser to
tighter counsel

4
Getting out more info as
speech proceeds

5
Moving from ease
to intensity

The overall audience response of this intensity may be contempt. Some listeners wonder if the high-decibel preacher really feels that strongly about everything he or she says. The audience suspects that the preacher is faking intensity. They may conclude that the preacher's passion is not genuine. Unrelenting passion is usually only a rhetorical style! This is the worst possible conclusion that an audience can make. Once passion is seen as a "preacher's tone," the whole subject looks bland.

Also, a second curse that emotionalism lays on some listeners is a feeling of shame. Listeners may incriminate themselves asking, "Why have I never felt as intense as the preacher does about this?" This kind of feeling can be very destructive. Why? Because they really need what the speaker is describing.

Being Sensitive

Those who know how to step over the ego barrier probably would sum up this chapter in two words: Be sensitive. Perhaps these two words derive from the Golden Rule. At the beginning of every sermon, the preacher should mentally change places with those who sit before him. He or she would then go a long way toward stepping over the ego barrier. Those who have served the same congregation for a long time have wrestled with many emotional entanglements. As a pastor, I found my own emotional involvement in persons' lives my greatest barrier in stepping over my own needs to reach out to others. This hyper-consciousness never led me to gloat over how I could use the audience for my own ends; rather, it was a selfishness of default. I became so wrapped up in some church problems that I could not shake myself free. I found I could not easily untangle myself from church administration. I thought about the burdens which the flock carried to worship. The only solutions that I have ever found to setting myself free enough to see others came from spiritual disciplines. Their sermon needs were answered by my own devotional habits. Only as I spent time with God could I shake free from the thrall that my own woes held over me.

In my earlier book on preaching, I talked about an exercise that I called *breaking*.[24] For me, this breaking was all-important if I was going to get out of myself Only as I escaped from me was I really able to see oth-

Breaking

The art of becoming human in a speech or sermon by cutting short the study of the speech with an unrelated activity

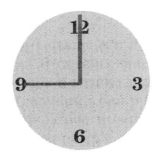

The Orator   **The Communicator**

ers and to deliver my sermon on their behalf. By "breaking," I meant I had to leave the study fifteen minutes before the gathering came to order. I needed this time to wander through the audience. In this aisle-roving maneuver, I listened, talked, and greeted others. As I did this, they also greeted me, sometimes in hurried, one-line phrases. Sometimes they quickly spoke to me of deep-seated needs that had brought them to church. Though it did not take long to amble through the audience it enabled me, by sermon time, to step out of my own emotional web and become one with them. Then I could speak to them. Whatever it takes, stepping over the ego barrier is the *sine qua non* of great preaching.

Unless we transcend the ego, we remain so shut up within ourselves that we do not deserve the name of Christian communicator.

Key Three:

Promising Your Hearers
Usable Information
and Keeping
Your Promise with Content

There is something glows upon my cheek,

and whispers in mine ear "Stay till he speak." [25]

The Audience Challenge
of
Key Three

Dear Speaker:

I hear a lot of people like you. I don't mean to be impertinent, but give me one good reason why I should listen?

Are you about to say something that I would find useful? Are you willing to promise me that if I do listen, I will hear something of consequence?

Exactly what kind of promise would I like you to make?

Promise me that I will be a different person after I have heard your words.

Promise me that after I have listened, I will upgrade my bogus values, jettison my impure motives, and commit myself to something glorious and dangerous and heady and wonderful.

Promise me that all the time I sit listening and you stand talking that I will see things I was unwilling to face before you preached. Help me see my sin, or God's glory, or Jesus' power.

Promise me that I, who am riddled with inferiority, will at last believe in myself.

I have always been afraid of heights. Challenge me with Everest. Promise me that after your words, I will be able to scale those icy walls and with God's help plant His mighty flag on the summit of all my doubts.

Promise me that I at last will know who I am and what I was born to achieve.

Promise all this and you shall have first my ear . . . and then my soul.

—Your Audience

The third communication key is the preacher's promise to give the audience usable information. Key Three communication is a little harder to locate and develop than the first two. It requires that we state the all-important communicating promise. It is generally wise to be forthright but never come on too strong. An audience is generally suspicious of such openings as "In the next few minutes I'm going to tell you the best news you've ever heard!" This kind of beginning sounds like a door-to-door vacuum-cleaner salesman.

"Why should I listen?" This question in traditional church settings should never be asked in this way. The pastor who addresses the same crowd each week must find creative ways to make the promise. The issue of "why should I listen?" may be well defined in the common vision of the church. Still, the question is not entirely unnecessary. Such an all-defining promise should only be assumed if the church is customarily filled with people and growing.

Why would I say this? Because only in full or growing churches is the church's vision this clearly defined. In the rapidly growing church, the people know why they are there. They know why they should listen. Pastors of these churches have consistently preached vital sermons. Their listeners come each week knowing what they are going to be told. The rapidly growing church has one defining message. That message is consistently preached, week after week, for the same vital reasons. Even without a Key Three promise, these attendees know one thing: They are going to hear, Sunday by Sunday, the restatement of the same driving vision.

Most mega-churches are marked by this kind of spirit. Their unifying, self-proclaiming vision is rarely written down. It hovers in the air of Sunday morning. None need reiterate the vision. All know what it is. The driving vision may be defined in this way: If anyone can sit in a church for fifteen minutes without being be able to tell what is important to that church, the church itself doesn't know what it thinks is important. The sermonic passion of growing churches consistently says, "This morning I am going to give you the same usable information I gave you last week. This speech like those before it will contribute to our whole reason to be. It is the mortar of our community."

When this principle is adhered to, there is constant vitality. On a regular basis, that vigorous *raison d'être* keeps answering the question, "Why should I listen?" This energy is based on one of two things. First, the corporate vision may have the Key Three promise written into it. Second, it may be that the word *relevant* has come to characterize the sermonic style of the visionary preacher.

Why Should We Listen?

Relevance is the real issue of Key Three preaching. Relevant content is so hard to find in most public speeches these days that the Key Three promise always needs to be made.

Application and relevance are absolute necessities in our day regardless of sermon type. A sermon, however harmonious its parts, however happy its structure, must touch people where they live . . . Great sermons do great good . . . they light the way in the dark for stumbling men.[26]

Relevance precedes application. People only apply sermons that have clear meaning for their lives. As an example of what we are talking about, let us turn to the advertising world and in particular to movie promotions. Generally at movies, before the feature presentation, we are shown "clip previews" from upcoming films. Theater managers want us to come back. What they are doing in such promotion is answering the question, "Why should I see this upcoming film?"

Films, it seems to me, are advertised in three general ways: they are advertised as important, entertaining, or classic. Can we transfer these words directly from movies to the sermon? If so, how? Is there a direct correlation between these three words and the question, "Why should I listen to you?"

Is It Important?

Let's look at these words one at a time, beginning with the word *important*. When a film is billed as important, it says to the audience, "This movie contains information that is necessary to the culture in general and to the individual viewer in particular." The implication: refusing to see this film will leave viewers deprived. The film has important information to share. Non-viewers condemn themselves to live forever in their own self-imposed ignorance.

Consider the film *Guess Who's Coming to Dinner*. This film was billed at the time by the theater industry as important. Why? Because the film was the first that introduced that last bastion of integration: interracial marriage. Martin Luther King and the civil rights movement had paved the way for an openness between the races. Some real progress had been made. But many still doubted that interracial marriage would work. There can be little question that the film *Guess Who's Coming to Dinner* was an important film. It helped many people become open to this new and important threshold in race relations.

Occasionally, there is a legitimate need to apply this word *important* to a sermon. A case in point may be a sermon I preached during the military build-up of the Desert Storm operation. This One-Hundred-Hour War was preceded by a time of edgy military stress. I was often called in by various families to pray for them. Their sons and daughters had already left to go to war. The anxieties of these families gathered around the maniacal threats of Saddam Hussein. This Iraqi madman woke all the fearsome, sleeping demons of the Third Reich.

This squeamish time of national nerve was also an edgy time for our church. Some thirty people from our congregation were involved in Desert Storm in one way or another. Amid tears, the families of our church had been separated by the dogs of war. I, too, felt discouragement as their children left home; they went off to be involved in a potentially long and dangerous conflict. Saddam Hussein was threatening the use of nerve gas and rocketry to wipe out all our American forces. In the midst of our congregational turmoil, I announced one Sunday morning that the evening service would contain an important sermon. I told them that I would not preach from the Bible. Instead I would be preaching from the Koran on the faith of Saddam Hussein.

I promised them the sermon would be important, and I prepared accordingly. The church attendance that night still remains the largest Sunday evening crowd in the history of the church. Why? Because this was an important sermon. Without this sermon the congregation would have remained unenlightened. I offered them a critical word they needed to hear to live through an uncertain time.

That sermon reinforced one truth in my mind. We preachers sin when we fail to notice those community or national issues that are pressing down on our people. I was haunted the night of my "Saddam Hussein sermon" for I wondered how many other relevant opportunities I had missed. Had I passed other significant seasons of congregational need without seeing them? Isn't looking at the needs of our audience a key step of audience analysis? Many Sundays preachers ought to give a film-clip of an upcoming sermon. People need urgent and informed reasons to come to church.

Is It Entertaining?

There is a second word that we ought to borrow from the motion-picture industry. The film world's advertising milieu also uses the word *entertaining*. This word does not carry the heavy advertising agenda of the word *important*. Still, the word entertaining suggests that the agenda for the film will keep our attention and require nothing much of us. The whole point of these movies (usually comedies, romance, or high-action) is that they will give us an absorbing break in the middle of our hassled lives. Such movies "rest us up." They are a kind of balm to heal the drab, killing, heavy routines of life.

We have already examined the use of humor in chapter 2; still let us be reminded that humor is a function of entertainment. Even the most important and prophetic sermons need a time of release from their demanding agenda. Humor well serves this need by breaking the content with a chance to enjoy the lighter aspects of a sermon's truth. It should be neither mere entertainment nor unrelated lightness. It should be tied naturally to the argument of the sermon. But it can be a happy resting point between heavy blocks of logic. Thomas G. Long has said it well: "No discerning person can stand in this place [the pulpit] in front of the community of Christ without a deep sense of awe and responsibility. It is also true that no one should stand in this place without a deep sense of humility and a healthy sense of humor."[27]

The entertainment value of a film is powerful. It prompts our friends to ask us, "Have you seen such-and-such film?" This question usually implies that they already have! In movie going it is always the best to own that little edge of power that comes from being the first on your block to have seen any film. "Well," they go on, "this movie is really enjoyable." The adjective for important movies is educational. The adjective for entertaining movies is enjoyable.

Is it possible to transfer such an easy and irresponsible word to a sermon? Isn't the word *entertaining* a bit lacking in dignity for the important work that sermons are called to do? Sermons should never be promoted as solely entertaining. Still, it doesn't hurt once in a while to have the word *entertaining* applied. There is implicit in entertainment the idea of rest. If public speaking cannot lay upon the audience some driven need to change the world, maybe it would at least be good to leave them a little more rested than when they came in.

Pearl Bailey led the all-African-American Broadway production of *Hello, Dolly*. Often after those fatiguing performances, she would come out, sit on the front part of the stage, and take questions from the audience. In one question-and-answer session, someone asked her why she went on with the grueling work of performing the same play night after night. She answered them in terms of the real value of entertainment: rest. She reminded them of Jesus' words in Matthew 11:28, "Come unto me, all ye that labor and are heavy laden, and I will give you rest." She was convinced that she needed to make tired, beleaguered New Yorkers laugh. If she could give them laughter and a little rest, she was convinced her calling to be rich.

Richard Foster, in another context, labeled our hassled executive schedules as the heavy "burden of getting ahead." Even if sermons never exist for the virtue of entertaining people, wouldn't it be nice if our speech helped people lay aside the heavy burden of getting ahead?

In terms of churchmanship, let us concede this: the sabbath principle of rest and the Hollywood idea of entertainment do, in a sense, pass close. The church is generally seen as an armory where we outfit people for the battle of life. Still it would be nice if we also saw the church as a hospital where Christians rested up to gain enough strength to reenter the battle. Wouldn't a little sermonic fun time help people want to come to church? Would they not come to church more eagerly if they saw in worship a brief respite from the heavy circumstances of their lives? Perhaps a bit of Pearl Bailey's sabbatarianism would help.

Is It Classic?

The third word that movie promoters use is *classic*. This is a word like the word *important*. The word *classic* implies that this movie will become a part of the human lore that defines the race. If you miss this classic film, you will have missed the finish. The word *classic* suggests that this film not only defines the best of the industry but it is also expected to endure through all time. This is another *Gone with the Wind*. Of course, film-makers never know if a new release will become a classic, as the press releases proclaim. The early 1990s remake of *The Last of the Mohicans* was advertised as a classic. Cooper's novel fits the term. But what of the movie? In a decade, we'll know if the advertising hype was prophecy or mere promotion.

It is unwise indeed to prophesy that your sermon will be a classic. It is far more likely that the endurance of the piece will pass away in time. Maybe it will be forgotten by Monday. Nonetheless, doesn't the word *classic* imply a specialness? Classic Coke is a particular kind of cola. So is the classic car or the classic novel. Each of them have been produced carefully and have wide acceptance and appeal. In this sense, sermons should be conceived of as classic even if they are never announced as such. Seeing the sermon as classic will cause the speaker to prepare it in a special way. Its content, its delivery, its very meaning to the audience will all be special. The speaker does not prepare this discourse as "one of the bunch." It is singular and more noble of purpose than the rest.

What causes a sermon to be viewed by the congregation as classic? It must address either a classic doctrine or use classic illustrations. For instance, I might illustrate a sermon on mercy with Portia's speech from *The Merchant of Venice*. The sermon itself might not be classic but it would sound classic because of the way I illustrated it.

On the other hand, if I preach a classic idea like incarnation but illustrate it with something from a Tom and Jerry cartoon, I spoil the classic feel of my argument. Classic is as classic does; better, classic is as classic sounds. There is an elite wholeness in the classic sermon as there is in classic music. In either, the finesse may not be interrupted with the banal or the whole mystique collapses.

The Functions of Relevance

Important
If you miss this sermon you will trivialize some portion of your life

Entertaining
If you miss this sermon you may live through your faith system too uptight to enjoy it

Classic
If you miss this sermon you will miss enduring truth

Examine how any sermon is to be prepared and promoted. You will see this idea is relative to the third communication key. Key Three promises them that, if they will listen, we will expound to them usable information. This sermon will be loaded with good content. Promoting our sermons is never wrong if we advertise them honestly. Honesty in advertising is all-important. The integrity of our promise means everything. We must live up to all we promote.

Creating a sense of vision for the audience will greatly enhance Key Three communication. Vision is the most obvious mark of great communication. Our speech must cause people to see themselves in particular ways. Once the sermon's vision is established, it should glue audience rapport together. The completed picture of what they will be after they appropriate the message should be clear to them. Their vision should drive the intensity of their interest.

Visionless sermons cannot create Key Three oratory. Aren't visionaries by definition persons of contagious agendas? They rarely come along. But here and there they appear. Visionaries almost give us a seeable finish line. Great sermons say, "Dream with me. My dreams are vital!" George Barna says, "A mark of a great leader is the ability not only to capture the vision, but also to articulate it and cause people to fully embrace it."[28] You have only to talk with real visionaries for a moment before they tell you how they feel about their role in the world. They are always evangelistic. They are out to tell you how their dreams can be applied to your own world. Visionaries always know where they are going. Direction and achievement define both their lives and their speeches. It is a wonderful gift they give to all who attend their words. Never ask visionaries how they are doing unless you really want to know. For them, all life is a crusade. They are leading it, and they believe you should be a part of it.

We have been looking largely at the motivating

beliefs of local pastors and their congregations. Let us now turn our attention to those occasions when we must address ourselves to being heard by people who don't know us. For these we need to assume that the Key Three promise is an integral part of our being heard.

Stating the Promise

How do we approach audiences unfamiliar with our preaching? The theme of such sermons will often have been announced in promotional brochures. They may even be supplied in a program folder which accompanies the occasion. Many times they are so well known that we expect them to speak from their reputed expertise. When this is the case, the theme of the meeting will seem preannounced. In such cases not much, if anything, really needs to be said of making a Key Three promise. But where does it need to be said? Two considerations need to be kept in mind. First, the promise should be stated in such a way that everyone understands that it is the single point of the communiqué. Second, the promise should be stated as briefly as possible. Let's look at these issues one at a time.

Making the Promise the Single Point of the Sermon

This premise is based on a singular bias: most sermons should have only one point. A three-point communiqué has two points too many. Fred Craddock says if a message does not have a single point then the preacher "does not have a single sermon, but three or four sermonettes, each related to the other as pegs on a board."[29] Three-point sermons tend to split themselves apart into three separate orations. Worst of all, they confuse the listener as to which of the three points is most important. The Key Three principle is really conditioned upon the sermon's having only one point to make. The preacher must state that point. This single-point promise then undergirds the presentation.

The 3-Point Sermon
and
The 1-Point Sermon
and

THE ISSUE OF DIRECTION

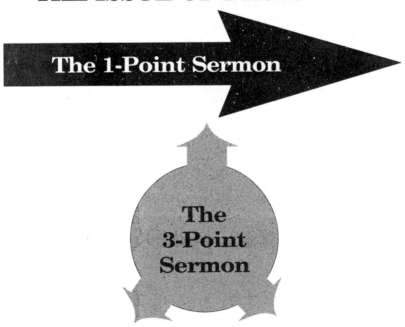

Making the Promise Short

How is the promise of usable information to be stated? In a word: briefly. Gathering a sermon around a single theme creates a kind of oratorical logo. This logo is a brief phrase which states the single purpose of the message. Al Fasol refers to this as "the major objective of the sermon." It is "a statement of what the preacher hopes to accomplish with this one message, from this one text, for this one congregation, or this one particular time."[30] The sermon logo, stated upfront, might be phrased like this:

- "This morning I want to give you the key to understanding your moods."
- "For years I suffered from not understanding why I could never find personal peace. Today, I am going to tell you something that might end that same struggle in your own life."
- "Should you be totally happy at work? Is your company healthy when you don't speak up? I'm going to answer these questions for you out of a basic look at your childhood."

One of the best talks I ever heard was given by an old man named Ralph Greensby. He had come into Oklahoma as a sodbuster and had begun to farm the land when "nary a plough-point had gouged the prairie." Ralph stood rather unceremoniously and said, "I want to tell you a truth that I learned many years ago when I first came into this cussed country. What I learned changed my life. I know it can change yours too." He began to relate the tale of his coming into Indian territory and staking his claim. He related the hardness of those early settlers and what they learned about the necessity of faith. While the old man talked, I was fascinated. What he learned about

Christ had changed his life. Somehow these forty years later his promise is still kept; my life was changed by his words and what he shared with me that day.

There are plenty of promotional speakers who emphasize the point. Almost all of them begin by saying something like this: "In the next few minutes, I am going to help you revolutionize the way you see your importance in your company." This promise becomes the sermon's gearbox. It moves the speaker (as we said in Key Two) across the ego barrier and toward the audience.

Now in sermonic terms, the promise might go something like this. "In the next few minutes I'm going to tell you how you may be able to end your depression." This promise should not be overstated. It should be a gentle, coercing force that makes the preacher live up to the pledge. The promise itself does not need to be continually repeated; the substance of the promise, however, should force the sermon to stay on track. What purpose does logo serve? What is its very mission to the speaker and the audience? Listeners should never be given a chance to forget the point of the speech. It is better to risk redundancy than to let the sermon's theme slip away.

The other aspects of Key Three will be covered as we determine to keep the promise. There are three pragmatics of doing this. First, we should make the promise reasonable. Second, we should surround it with hard-hitting content. And third, we should wrap up the deal by mentioning the promise we have kept. This last step will not be one where we say, "Aha, I told you so!" It will be rather a step we take to resolve listener tension. With step three we complete our communiqué. Let us now address these three aspects of keeping the sermon's promise: making it reasonable, the four forms of content, and the wrap.

Making It Reasonable

Reasonable Means Logical

Before a Key Three promise can be reasonable to an audience, it must pass a fourfold test. The first test of reason asks, "Is it logical?" This test of the promise means that listeners must be able to see why you made the promise. They must be able to figure out what you are saying. They certainly must be able to figure out what the message is about.

Only a couple of things will guarantee this. First, can the speaker put herself in the audience's shoes? Can she separate herself from all that she knows about her subject and imagine that she is hearing the subject for the first time? If she can, she can make her presentation in a key way, answering the issues her content raises. I must make this point once again: presumption is a killer. It sins by taking for granted that the audience knows more about the subject than they really do. It is unwise to presume they are informed. It is better to tell them something they already know than to neglect to tell them what they need to know.

In fact, planned redundancy may be the way we best teach. How often Jesus repeated himself when teaching His disciples! Was He absentminded? Did He not realize He had already told them these same truths before? Then why again? Because great truths can never be redundant. Further, repetition is the key to remembrance.

Often I hear black preachers who gather their communiqués about simple themes. They may repeat these logos a score of times throughout their sermons, yet I do not hear these repetitions as redundant. They are emphatic, repeated, and crafted calls to remembrance.

Is there anything that can guarantee a logical format in such preaching? Just this: Fidelity to a detailed outline along which the oft-stated theme of the sermon proceeds. The outline is there forcing us to move directly and logically through the dissemination of content. Nothing is left out. What ends does this format serve? It liberates the speaker to control a well-ordered agenda.

How glorious this liberty is. John Broadus celebrates this freedom: "Whether in preparation or in delivery of sermons, a man's feelings will flow naturally and freely only when he has the stimulus, support, and satisfaction which come from conscious order."[31] If such order is omitted, mobility dies. And logic has for its most important function mobility. It

The Two Basic Rules of Mobility

1 LOGIC *Flies*

2 DISORDER Plods

makes the speech move! When the sermon comes at us in a logical fashion we feel that we are moving. But when the sermon meanders a rabbit-chasing way, we feel as if we are lost in a house of mirrors. We travel past familiar vistas of unrelated scripture-scapes, and we know we are lost! Two simple rules explain a sermon's mobility: Logic flies, and disorder plods.

I remember a dreadful day in Boston when I was trying to take my family to see the Old North Church. We kept going past it on the freeway. I could look over the side of the freeway and see it. I would then whiz past it, get off at the next exit, and try to drive approximately to where I thought it was. Just when I would feel that I was almost there, I was somehow back on the entrance ramp to the freeway. Once again I would go whizzing past the Old North Church. My sensation was always the same: I was in a sense showing my children the church, but I knew they weren't getting the full historic impact of it. They were glimpsing the spire as they sped past it at fifty-five miles per hour.

What bothered me the most was the feeling that I had delivered some sermons like that. I had also heard a few like that. How very often speakers lead us whizzing past the same oratorical vistas. We never really locate their message because they never locate their point. The word that describes this situation is lost. At such a place in communication the whole audience is lost. But what is it that is really lost when redundancy haunts a sermon? Mobility. And what happens when mobility mires down in heavy boots? Confusion and chaos. The best truth is never pedestrian. It is ever nimble on its feet.

Reasonable Means Applicable

Much of what we are saying has to do with relevance. Sermons have no relevance until the listener can apply them to life. It is most difficult, however, for a speaker to say anything which will apply with equal usability to everyone in the audience. This is particularly true of sermons delivered to different age-groups. Such discourse severely challenges relevancy. How is the preacher to make the subject real to such a varied constituency? How is it possible to preach to everyone from the local mechanic to the thoracic surgeon? From the five-year-old to the retiree? The application must be kept within reach of all.

Reasonable Means Within Reach

This struggle to relate the Bible to life is called relevance. The issue of content in our preaching must deal with one question: Can they reach it? Martin Luther had a wonderful rule for keeping things simple. He believed that when you set a discourse within the reach of the simplest you will have set it within the reach of all. Luther was once asked how he managed to speak with interest to the smartest people in Germany—to all the doctors and professors of his congregation. His classic reply was that most times he just preached to "Hansie and Betsy." The speech geared to reach the intelligent usually reaches no one, not even the intelligent! But the communiqué geared to reach the simple gives everyone access to its truth.

Perhaps this is a good place to stop and say that one way to hold interest is to sprinkle your sermons with children's stories and poems. Not only will the children then understand the sermon, but it will also enthrall adults as well. Disney's ever-circling popularity proves that adults love what children understand. The beauty of this approach is that all adults were once children. Their appreciation of simple stories never leaves them. On the contrary, however, children have never been adults, and thus adult illustrations elude them.

When I began to write children's books a decade ago, I discovered that the whole world was interested in them. Try this experiment, and you will doubtless prove the point: Read your favorite clip from Shakespeare in the same speech where you also tuck

The Word That Draws the Crowd

The Relevance Word

The Irrelevance Word

in a few of your favorite lines from Dr. Seuss. You will immediately see which holds the most compelling interest. Key Three communication says one thing clearly: if you want everyone in the audience to eat from your oratorical table, be sure the table is low enough. If the food you serve is unreachable, malnutrition will inhabit your speaking.

Reasonable Means Something They Can Appropriate Now

Reason and relevance, as we have said, are bedfellows. Relevance always asks two questions:
- Can I use this information?
- Can I use this information now?

Our generation is not only called the communication age, it is also called the "now" generation. Microwave ovens, instant banking, and fast-food testify that our generation is impatient. All the content of a speech must be usable right now.

The Four Forms of Content

Four very special, yet distinctive, forms allow us to build content. They interrelate, criss-cross, blend, fade, dissolve, and recouple in never-ending patterns of intrigue and rhetorical clout. In a very real sense, they cannot be studied separately nor can they be amputated into separate forms. Yet for the sake of clarity, let's consider each form in its own unique style.

The Precept—The Path of Reason

Although the forms we are going to examine are four, only two define the flow of the sermon. The first of these is precept—those statements which build the path of logic with a trackable style. Thomas G. Long observed: "Many names are used to describe the component parts of a sermon; points, moves, steps, episodes, units, and so on. Regardless of the label applied to the parts, a sermon consists of a series of segments arranged in a logical sequence."[32]

So precepts are statements which can be organized to give this logical flow. But if there is any integrity in the communiqué, the precept must be true. These statements must follow in some trackable order. They should be able to be outlined. Logical, procedural precepts form the matrix of simple argument. Into this matrix of procedural argument may be dropped other speaking forms to furnish the communiqué with interest.

Dropping a poem into the perceptual matrix, for instance, will furnish the sermon with music. Dropping a story into the precepts will furnish the sermon with intrigue. Dropping a quote into the argument will furnish the sermon with authority. Dropping an inductive lead (a question for self-examination) into the precepts will furnish the sermon with counseling. Dropping statistics into the matrix will furnish it with information. In certain circumstances, dropping a supporting Scripture into the precepts will furnish the dialogue with the voice of God. All such forms color, inform, and enforce our rhetoric with power. But well-ordered precepts will give the sermon movement and trackable logic.

The Statistics—The Path of Proof

It has often been said that statistics don't lie but that liars do use statistics. It is true that we can distort statistics to prove almost anything. Nonetheless, there is a certain authority in statistics that buttress sermonic force. The hardest question regarding statistics is this: "Where do we go to get them?" There seems to be no immediate source for the statistics we really need. We can hunt them down in books and magazines. *USA Today* and the newsmagazines abound with colored graphs, pie-charts, and percentage tables. Let's be wise as we read through these periodicals and clip what we may one day include in a speech. Statistics that really support specific rhetoric are hard to find. It is good, therefore, to gather statistics as we read from day to day.

Assuming, however, that we do have the statistics we need, there still remains the question of how much to use them. An audience is quickly debilitated with hard argument. Too many statistics smother argument rather than enhance it. The key rule is clarity. When you have used statistics to give your argument just the punch it needs, use some other rhetorical device to interpret the statistics.

For instance, consider a hypothetical speaker's use of statistics:

> Thirty-eight percent of New York's working mothers leave their children in day-care centers. Twenty-three percent of those left have not had adequate nutrition in the twelve hours that have elapsed since they last spent time there. But a staggering 84 percent of day-care workers have eaten no breakfast before their arrival at work. The mood established by all this poor nutrition leads 68 per-

cent of day-care certifying agencies to suggest that 33 percent of child-abuse cases may
be directly traceable to the 84-percent factor,
at least in 23 percent of the cases. Please
keep in mind there is a plus-or-minus 3 percent accuracy in these statistics.

Is your understanding helped by this factual pile-
up? These statistics get ignored because they are not
interpreted by some other rhetorical device. Statistics
should be used in conjunction with illustrations, quotations, precepts, and personal opinions. In fact, statistics are valueless to the listener unless some other
application makes them come alive. As Daniel O'Keefe
noted: "Studies in communication theory show that
the presentation of case studies with pertinent exam-
ples of individual experience are a much more effective means of communicating than are statistical sum-
maries."[33]
The statistics in the extract above need to be interrupted by a story to flesh them out with meaning. For
instance, "Mary Magillocutte began to notice small
blue marks on her daughter's wrists each evening
when she picked her up from The Happy-face Place, a
swank day-care center in lower Manhattan. . . ." This
story will illumine and reinforce the above statistics.
It enables them to serve. Stories and the statistics are
symbiotic. Each needs the other to assist in the making of a single point.

Story—The Path of Intrigue

Not much needs to be said about the story as a
source of content in a sermon. It is dealt with in detail

in this book and certainly in my earlier book *Spirit, Word, and Story*.[34] Story does need to take its rightful place in this list of content forms, however. No form is quite so important as this one. Nor is any aspect of public speaking more important than storytelling. Beyond doubt, the most saveable, "take-home-able," and "carry-through-life-able" aspect of any speech or sermon is the story.

Stories not only hold and communicate information, they are also the best of all forms for holding attention. In the next chapter we will look at Key Four, how to keep tension on audience interest. In this important matter nothing will serve as well as story. But stories do not merely hold interest; they also form a container to hold the content of the sermon. Christ's parables reinforce the idea that Christianity comes packaged in narratives. Never underestimate the force with which stories package truth. This force is so formidable that every public speaker should commit herself to learning all she can about narrative style. Ours is a story-soaked day. Our world is conditioned to love narrative forms. Totally narrative sermons are now welcome and expected. Any preacher who wants to preach to our age must permit our culture its love-affair with stories.

The Inductive Lead

In Key Three communication, the inductive lead and the promise of usable information may seem unrelated. But consider what Ralph Lewis has to say:

> Philosophers have found only two basic structures—inductive and deductive—for all human thought patterns. Why has preaching

concentrated on one and ignored the other? Do we expect our listeners to shut down half their brains on Sunday morning?[35]

Induction allows for selective sampling of the "sermon salad." Induction asks the listener to respond. It invites listeners to eat only those parts of the salad they like. But induction believes that no information is palatable unless the audience believes it is. The inductive lead encourages listeners to make up their own minds about the relevance of the communiqué. In an earlier chapter, we talked about the inductive style. Now let us consider how induction is the style of the best sermons.

An inductive lead is a promise couched in a question. In the past, sermonic promises were usually couched in threats or commandments: "My dear brothers and sisters, I am going to tell you in the next thirty minutes what you need to do to get right with God! All pussyfooting aside, you need to understand what God has to say to you about your sin life, and repent at once! Listen up, you brood of vipers!" The favorite verbs of yesterday's preaching were all imperatives. Its favorite pronoun was *you*. Its favorite punctuation, the exclamation point. Today's preaching, by contrast, has for its favorite mood the indicative. Its favorite pronoun is *we* and its favorite punctuation is the question mark.

The inductive lead gives listeners possible premises and lets them decide: "This morning, I would like to examine what the Bible has to say about sin. Will you, in your mind, search through this subject with me? If you are willing to do so in the next thirty minutes, you may be able to conclude exactly what your standing with God is." The inductive lead makes it clear to the audience that the sermon does not set out to enforce the Word of God in their lives. The sermon exists to counsel all with its appropriating truth. The inductive lead beckons them to enter into truth at their pace. The Key Three promise is put to them in gentler options that they decide upon.

The inductive lead permeates the best sermons with subtle interrogatives that invite their attention, their thinking, and their decisions. The key word is *invite*. The inductive lead pauses here and there throughout the presentation. It invites all to consider the next slice of rhetoric we will give them. As we said in chapter 2, we must get over the notion that even the speech is *ours*. We must cross the ego barrier and make the

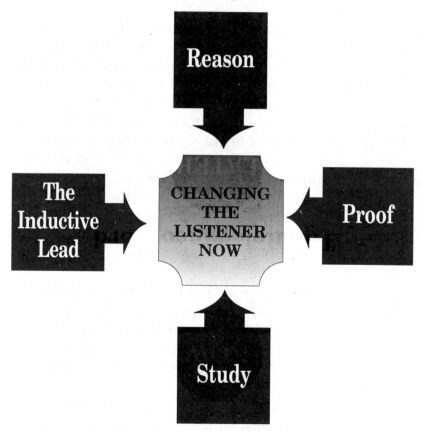

communication *theirs*. No technique will help to scale the ego barrier faster and more thoroughly than the inductive lead.

When a communicator is doing it right, the lead itself becomes second nature, and the speaker is unaware it is happening. Listeners become involved because they want to be. They decide because they want to decide. No sermon belongs to us until we give it to God. As long as we preach in imperatives, there is a strong likelihood that we have not fully distinguished between "thus sayeth the Lord" and "thus sayeth the preacher."

I will cover the matter of sermonic authority later. For the moment, let me say, good preaching still says, "Thus sayeth the Lord." We shouldn't force God to speak inductively. He may order us as He will. But we must be sure that all our thus-sayeth-the-Lords are taken from Scripture. Our audience should know clearly when God is speaking and when we are giving our own opinion. All the direct authority of our sermons should come directly from cited Scripture. Yet, even these should be surrounded by inductive leads that "invite" our hearers to consider the "demands of God."

All authority of the communiqué must come directly from strong biblical content. Triumphalism is never appropriate. Neither is any selfish desire to use people or situations for our own sake. We must never mix the force of rhetorical imperatives with the weakness of our own agenda. We should precede every proposition of the discourse with induction.

I don't mean to be sacrilegious, but egocentrism usually has a touch of phony godhood about it. We can deliver a sermon with a bogus baptism of passion. We sin when we need to control people or situations. Seeing ourselves as **Mr.** or **Ms.** **Right** attempts to squelch our opposition by using theatrical passion. Such personal pietism is fraught with dangers, for it supplants induction with papalism. Dan McBride used to sing a song that included the line, "This must be the will of the Lord because it seems so right to me." Presuming against the audience's right to dignity is an easy mistake. Still, it often begins when we think that we know beyond all doubt what is good for everyone. Such presumption filled the tubs of Jonesville with cherry Kool-aid. So let us guard ourselves against all audience manipulation. Using the inductive lead protects everyone, both the preacher and the audience.

The Wrap

To be sure that you have fully employed the Key Three technique you must pay final attention to the conclusion of the speech: the wrap. As the communiqué closes, you must do three things: you must restate the promise, show them how you kept it, and then ask them to firm up their final response. This wrap should let them tie together the sermon and help the audience take the package home.

There is a simplistic old outline from Speech 101 classes: "Tell them what you're going to tell them, tell them, and then tell them what you told them." This outline has some things to commend it. The word *told* may be a little strong for the inductive model we are suggesting, but otherwise the outline is a good description of how to make a one-point speech work well.

I often will repeat a short quote or a precept at the first of any sermon or lecture I give. Then I repeat the same quote at the conclusion as well. This helps ensure that the Key Three promise is examined at the first and last of a sermon and a few times en route. This impor-

The Three
I-Told-You-So Issues
of Preaching

1 THE PROMISE
What You're Going
to Tell 'Em

2 THE MESSAGE
Tell 'Em

3 THE WRAP
What You've Told 'Em

tant counsel must walk that very thin line between redundancy and emphasis. It requires a great deal of experience to know the proper level of reinforcing the premise.

Making and keeping a Key Three promise will be for some a new way of preaching. It may also prove to be a more effective way. For some, it will be a harder kind of communication to get used to. For still a third group, it may appear as awkward to the audience as it does the preacher. One thing is sure: we must not take the Key Three approach so seriously that it becomes a regimented form rather than a productive device. Yet this simple form preserves both the force of discourse and the dignity of the listener. No better compliment can be given to effective communicators. For to preach with force while we serve and save the dignity of our audience is the double blessing of Key Three communicators.

Key Four:

Creating Tension and Resolution:
Building Attention with Story
and Finishing with
A Happy Ending

My lord, you told me you would tell the rest,

When weeping made you break the story off.[36]

The Audience Challenge of
Key Four

Dear Speaker:

I really don't want to listen to you at all unless you wish to report that the building is on fire. Crises give me interest in those speeches that propose solutions. You're going to have to make your words appear vital somehow . . . it's a matter of tension.

Take the other night, for instance. There was a network documentary on burglary and violence. It was very boring so I turned off the television and went to bed. Then sometime after midnight, I was awakened by the chilling sound of breaking glass. When I looked in at the French doors that lead to the patio, I saw a huge, hairy hand reaching though the broken window, and turning the dead bolt . . . the door creaked open. The hair rose on the back of my neck, as the huge hulk of the intruder moved stealthily into the center of the room. I reached for the mace in my dresser drawer and stole quietly behind the antique wardrobe. I waited as the fiend approached. I crouched. My trembling forefinger was poised on the aerosol trigger. As he came past my hiding place, I rose and pressed the lever.

"PSSSSSSST!" hissed the can. The vapor shot into the evil face of the menacing marauder. The deadly fog found its way in the darkness. My would-be assassin fell comatose on the floor.

I turned on the light.

It was the Avon Lady.

I felt little remorse over what I had done. She should have used the doorbell and she should have come earlier in the day. Anyway, for a dreadful moment she had my attention. My nervous system was screaming. And I couldn't help but wonder why your sermons never leave me this breathless. When I am as rapt in the spell of your words as I was in that fearful moment of waiting, then I promise you I will listen. I won't be able to do anything else.

                                        —Your Audience

I am not a fisherman but fishing intrigues me. Catching the big one always involves the matter of tension. Sport reels have a tension mechanism that produces drag on the line which makes fishing a matter of "catching" and "releasing." The hooked fish is given a quasi-controlled freedom. He is always allowed periodic flights of escape even as he is pulled in until he succumbs in fatigue to these "flights." The fisherman is a master of tension. Slowly he draws the fish in, alternating tension and release. Alas, the poor fish is snuggled longitudinally in his creel. Lying silver-bodied with all his fatigued brothers and sisters, the fish realizes, at last, he was at the mercy of a skillful sportsman. He had met a technician, schooled in the principle of tension and release.

In a less devious way, Eugene Lowry has suggested the principle of the Lowry Loop. This loop is the tension-and-release mechanism of narrative preaching. The inductive process of narration supplies the techniques of tension through gentle induction. At last the listeners have arrived at their own conclusions.

The late Barbara Tuchman was a fascinating historian. During all the years she wrote, she hung one little sign over her typewriter: "Will the Reader Turn the Page?" Successful writers know that they must create a sense of suspense to capture readers and hold their attention.

Really great preachers do not create *attention*; they create *tension*. The tension comes from the speaker and the attention is conferred by the audience. Sermonic tension is born in the communicator's deter-

THE TENSION-AND-RELEASE SYNDROME

In the speaker's tension-and-release system, the audience is never quite set free. They are held captive within a system of apparent freedom.

mination. The audience must never relax at their caprice while the preacher is talking. Our words are too important to allow our audience to listen in a mentally slouchy mode. But beware: communicators must live in a tension even as they create it. The issue of audience tension gives rise to a big question: How do I maintain an easy, casual, demeanor while I lock them in passionate concern on the edge of their seats? This paradox is the preacher's milieu. Every spellbinder must keep a casual demeanor even as he creates that tension. The audience, like spring bass, must eagerly and hungrily snap at the words. In this chapter, we want to show how "casual" and "concerned" are speaker's contrivances.

There is a traceable pattern in which audience interest decays. Listeners begin to quit listening by slouching backwards in their seats. The next phase of interest decay is usually manifested in a sprawling posture. The third step of decay is seen in eyes that abandon their speaker-focus as their ears really have already done. As the eyes become bored, they begin to look around the room; then they notice that their fingernails haven't been filed in a while (probably since the last unexciting speaker that they heard). Finally their minds, agreeing with their other abdicating senses, jump ship. Only their dutiful bodies stay put. Their minds are far away on a long and well-deserved South Seas cruise. The not-so-communicative communicator talks on alone in his universe of bodies whose minds have been snatched away.

How do we keep such sermonic decay from occurring? Tension! Tension is that agitated state of our nervous system that is called disequilibrium. In any state of disequilibrium, we are doing all we can to move back into a state of balance.

Winters in Nebraska were characterized by months of icy roads and sidewalks. Needless to say, I have slipped and fallen on the ice a multitude of times. I don't mind walking upright on the ice. I don't even mind lying face down on the ice. What I do hate is that awkward, incorrectable state of falling. There is a state of existence when we are neither right-side up or faceside down. We are in disequilibrium. The futile cry of our souls in this limbo is anguish. Neither up nor down, we are possessed by a furious need for definition. Where are we? When will the crash reorient our lives? Will we break something? Will we hurt something? Will we look foolish? In the state of disequilibrium, all these thoughts run through our minds. It doesn't take much time to fall, yet it is such an eternity that our entire lives flash before us.

In the act of falling, we are never carefree. We are never bored. We are never disinterested. We are all attention. We care. How do we at last escape these categories? We hit the ground! We are down! Gravity, be praised! We are through being out of control. The problem is solved! But something is broken! Good, we'll have it fixed! Nothing is broken. Good, we don't need to have it fixed! All is rejoicing! The disequilibrium is over. Only a few people saw us make a fool of ourselves and they were all strangers. Great! What do we care if they are giggling and pointing! How happy and wonderful it feels to be through falling!

F. Scott Fitzgerald recognized this edge of the precipice disequilibrium: "Draw your chair up close to the edge of the precipice and I'll tell you a story."[37]

> F. Scott Fitzgerald was right; a good story invites us to the edge of a precipice. There we may be enshrouded in a dense cloud of fear with Anne Frank or breathe deeply the autumn-crisp air of freedom with Harriet Tubman or splash in crackling cold joy with Helen Keller. On the edge of the story precipice we can celebrate a wonderful party with a girl named Alice or fire the last shot from "Ol' Betsy" at the Alamo. A good story never bores. Balancing on the edge of a precipice brands the memory so that the story is often the only part of the sermon people will recall and try to recount to a friend.[38]

How clever the storyteller who keeps his audience "on the edge!" Gloriously unsettled, they learn the truths the exposition contains.

Recently I went to see the movie *Cliffhanger*. I dislike clichés, but I must say the movie was really awesome. The audience was riveted to the screen. Why? Because the film was not about climbing mountains; it was about falling off them. In various scenes, people who were trying hard to hang on, fell off. This disequilibrium made the film the most compelling I have ever seen.

During sermons, preachers usually know the disequilibrium of falling. They feel all the emotions that they would like their audiences to feel. They tumble out of control. Down, down they perish in a sea of yawning, absentee souls. The key to great preaching is for the preacher to create this state, not role model it. The communicator must create insecurity in listeners.

Eugene Lowry has become famous for his insights on that audience tension that the narrative sermon supplies. Stories can produce a suspense with a sermon that only releases the audience when the story is over. His loop indicates that the narrative sermon must not drive too directly for attention. The pace of the story must slow down to supply a little relief. The loop of the graphic demonstrates this. The good preacher builds a little rest into the narrative tension that keeps listeners on line without ever letting them go. The loop is relief, not relinquishment.

This tension-release mechanism must operate all through the sermon. To keep a rope on an audience,

LOWRY'S LOOP

MOTIVATED LISTENING

we must destroy the listeners' equilibrium. In this agitated state, they listen. Professor Harold Hill, in Meredith Wilson's *Music Man*, whips the good citizens of River City, Iowa, into a frenzy. He feeds upon their paranoia. He points out that the newest thing to enter River City is a pooltable. In this wonderful melodrama, Harold Hill introduces tension and disequilibrium. The good townsfolk of River City thought they were happy. Alas, they are made aware of a grave demon in their midst. What can the moral infection of a pooltable mean in a small town? What will happen in River City? Who knows? They have not hit the ground yet, but their small town security has been displaced by disequilibrium. They must now focus hard on the subject at hand. Professor Harold Hill may be a charlatan; he may be a shyster, but he is not boring!

Tension may be built in two ways: first, by using stories, and second, by using suspense and revelation. Let's turn our attention to the first of these devices.

Story Narration

Four forms illustrate (or literally "cast light on") communication. The first form is an example, which may or may not be narrative in quality. The second, illustration, is just an example that has grown more detailed to more thoroughly illustrate a point. A third is the anecdote, which is a brief story, often humorous, that binds a perceptual point to a running tale to make the precept clearer and more memorable. The fourth form, narrative, is a longer and more involved story. Narratives not only make clear some important

THE FOUR ILLUSTRATION FORMS

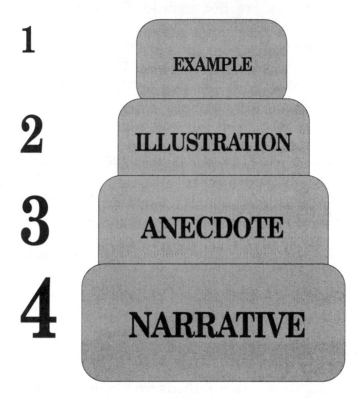

1   EXAMPLE

2   ILLUSTRATION

3   ANECDOTE

4   NARRATIVE

point, but because they tell long stories they have the possibility of enforcing the sermon's logic while holding the hearer's attention.[39]

The story as a major sermon emphasis has become common in the communication age. Sidney Greidanus believes the importance of the sermonic story was born around 1970.[40] Whenever it began, it is now an established sermon form. This form of communication has amazing importance in our video-soaked generation.

We all love stories because they fill life with movement. We have already said that we don't find sermons interesting because they lack mobility. Far too often, sermons are exhibits that we walk around, but they themselves are not mobile. Stories move sermons and the motion intrigues.

Narrative creates the glorious tension of lost equilibrium. Think of the thousands of times of story-driven tension you have felt. Will Benji Engie ever get over the hill, even if he thinks he can? Will Lassie make it home even if she thinks she can? Can Beauty stand to kiss the Beast even though his ugliness freezes her blood? Will Superman ever reveal his real identity to that vixen, Lois Lane? Can Elmer Gantry ever triumph over his flirtatious passions? Must Uriah Heep destroy David Copperfield? Will Anna Karenina really throw herself under the train? These considerations are enough to tell us that stories are important to sermons. While the tension of such stories are on us, we are in disequilibrium.

Augustine's Narratio

It was Augustine, that famous first homiletician, who advanced the idea of the sermon as *narratio*. The sermon as a story survives best when the individual component stories of the communiqué merge in their relatedness. This gathering of tales then communicates the single, larger point of the sermon. The individual illustrations of our communiqué must not become too separate in theme. When this happens you arrive at a hodge-podge *narratio*, one that is too diverse to bear a single, strong thread of tension.

Augustine, in speaking in a broader way on the sermon put it this way:

Ita dicere delsere eloquentem, ut doceat, ut delectat, ut flectat—a speaker should express himself in such a way that he teaches, that he attracts, that he turns (moves the hearer).[41]

It is this attracting quality of the story that snags the listeners and compels them to listen.

But do not push the principle. It is not necessarily true that if one story interests an audience, twenty will awe them. Each individual story will gig attention, but the endless piling of story upon story sooner or later does just the opposite. When stories mesh pointlessly together, they no longer trap our attention. They mire our souls in gunky, meaningless plots. The trick is to have the sermon's individual illustrations well spaced by precepts, quotes, reasonings, statistics and other blocks of logic. When this integration occurs, then all the illustrations will serve. Several stories can each take part in the single *narratio* that enforces tension to the sermon's end.

There can be little doubt as to the rhetorical force of stories. But let us not narrow their significance till we see them as a rhetorical lure. Story is not there to coerce innocent listeners into our narrative net where we may gig them with some great hermeneutical trident. Mircea Eliade called humankind *homo religiosus*. This Latinism is more than just "religious man." John Newport says this is man hungry for the transcendent.[42]

Stories that apply ultimate force are those which speak to our ultimate hungers. These stories hold interest not just because they create tension and disequilibrium. They are ultimate because they describe the deepest passions of our existence.

But how are we to first establish the *narratio*? How

are we to arrive at the resolution to the tension that leaves our hearers at peace? Two conditions must be met before we bring a story to an end.

The Unresolved Plot: The Entire Sermon as One Story. The issue of when to end the tension rests on two considerations. First, the tension should end when the argument is complete. We must not end before we have told them all they need to know. It is the bane of the evangelical sermon that we talk so long but finish so short of what we set ourselves to accomplish. We almost always finish our sermons before we equip listeners to do what our message has challenged them to do! For churches that have an altar call, this is a neurotic short-coming. Why neurotic? Because many preachers believe their success or failure depends on whether anyone comes to the altar. The reason people don't come forward often has nothing to do with the quality of communication. The problem is that we finish the sermon before we've given them all the information they need. They may feel motivated to come forward but they don't understand why they need to make a decision. Or, even if they feel a need to come forward, they don't know exactly what they need to do once they are at the altar.

Often we cover the sermon's too-quick ending by granting ourselves a spiritual out. We are prone to say, "The Spirit wasn't working among us very well today" or "The congregation is so secularly oriented they can't deal with the deep spiritual issues of my sermon." The real truth is that we haven't given them all the information they needed. If we had, they might have made the decisions we wanted them to make.

The issues of why preachers fail to give listeners all the information they need rests on two primary faults. The first fault proceeds from this assumption: everybody knows about what I know. The second is a presumption: those who will not make a decision are hard of heart.

Let's deal first with the assumption that everyone knows about what I know. This assumption is never meant to congratulate ourselves or put down anyone else. This assumption grows quite naturally from the center of our worldview. It is easy to project our worldview onto the demeanor of our listeners. The projection issues not from egocentrism, but from a more innocent self-preoccupation. We continually talk to ourselves in those egocentric, unceasing mental conversations that gobble up our years. What we practice inwardly, we come to feel is common parlance. Thus, we never see the need of explaining to others what we feel they must know because we know it so well.

But in addition to this grand (and false) assumption we are also guilty of spiritual presumption. Preachers especially sin this way. When parishioners do not readily make decisions, preachers think them hard-hearted. "If only they would yield to Christ," such preachers say to themselves, "then they could develop a radiant walk of faith." In actuality, the real reason that their congregants don't come forward is not an issue of disobedience. We have closed the sermon before we gave them the necessary information they need to follow Christ.

The Resolution Is Twofold. In more secular realms of public speaking, however, lessening audience tension should not be done until the speech is completely over. One of the most obvious and least intentional ways we lessen the tension is in body language. The bodily energy we expend is spent in direct relationship to the amount of audience tension we hold. When the passion of the discourse is at a maximum, interest is also at a maximum. But when the energy track of our mood is allowed to relax, the audience begins to relax.

Energy levels are sustained by what I call the inner, magic camera. We must visualize at every moment of our delivery how we appear in this magic camera. If we see our energy slipping, we must goad our psyches to a higher plateau of animation. We must never take our mental eye away from that magic camera. Only then can we watch ourselves perform. If we forget to watch ourselves perform, we will ease up on the communication force. We will then "casual" away the earnestness of our delivery.

Good communication means that we are always keeping one track of our inner camera focused on our performance. The other track of our camera's eye must be focused on their reception of what we're saying. The first track of the camera gives us feedback as to how we're doing in our opinion. The second track of the camera lets us know how we're doing in their opinion. When both cameras are getting the proper read-out, audience tension should remain adequate.

But the most obvious way of lessening interest is to "give away" our tension by actually telling them that the sermon is soon to end. It will also occur when we say, stuttering like Porky Pig, "That's all, folks!" This devastating benediction is seldom recoverable. Therefore, I offer you the three never-never rules regarding the last minutes of the sermon. Consider carefully the first.

The first never-never rule is this: Never give them a progress report as to where you are in your delivery. This, by the way, is the greatest weakness of the three-point sermon. This manner of outlining always gives them a feeling of knowing just how far along you are in the sermon. As you near point three, they ready themselves to quit listening. One-point preaching circumvents this problem.

However, you may report where you are in your delivery in many other ways. The first never-never rule is usually violated when the preacher says, "one more observation and I'm through," or "As I close, pay special attention," or "Now as I close, let me reiterate," or "I want to give you five facets of my argument and a brief wrap-up." All such statements release audience tension. You are telling your audience to get ready to stop listening.

A second never-never rule is this: Never anti-climax your final point. Never pass up your dramatic, final, stopping place. This is often evidenced by preachers who have a preference for impressive stories to conclude their sermons. Grasping this illustrating megapower to your gripping conclusion means you must stop when the awe settles. Let the lingering drama of that illustration be taken home from church by those who attend the sermon. To "murk" the grandeur with

---

THE THREE
NEVER-NEVER RULES

NEVER

- **Give them a progress report as to where you are in your sermon**

- **Anti-climax a dramatic conclusion with weaker commentary**

- **Extend the sermon beyond the slackening of communicative tension**

---

further comment damages the finale. To go on talking for a long time after the grandeur is past obliterates it.

The third never-never rule has to do with the wholeness of the communiqué: Never extend the sermon beyond that point where the tension relaxes. When the tension is lifted, the argument must conclude. To further extend a very commanding sermon will only see it dawdle to a drowsy and imprecise ending.

Suspense Before Revelation

The use of story, of course, is not the only way to build audience tension. There are many other ways this can be accomplished. Let's quickly rehearse three of them.

Building to Apocalypse. The apocalypse manner of creating tension is found in the root meaning of the word *revelation*. The word *revelation* has the idea of drawing the drapes. It suggests a pulling of that curtain which allows an audience to see a play. At the unveiling of a statue, there is considerable audience interest until the cord is clipped and the veil falls away. Then the hidden becomes obvious.

At the center of great sermons lies some portent of truth about to be revealed. Through a spellbinding argument, logic is laid down, and the hidden is hinted at. Then at the appropriate time, the curtain is drawn and the revelation is laid open. The suspense ends and so does the speech.

Some years ago, I heard a young preacher promise me (and the rest of the audience) that he was going to show us the most dangerous weapon in the world. At the beginning of his argument he produced a large sack. The first long, curved object he drew out of the sack was a machete. He swung the blade about him. He set it singing through the air like the sword of a samurai. He told us of all the historical exploits of the sword. As he did, he once again made the blade slice the electric air like a saracen scimitar. But when he was finished with it, he laid it calmly to one side and said, "Alas, this is not the most dangerous weapon in the world."

He went back to the sack. This time he drew out a hand gun—a real pistol. It was filled with blanks and he fired it into the air. The report of the pistol caused all to jump in fright. Once more he talked about all the dastardly things that had been done with pistols through the ages. He rehearsed the crimes of Capone, the rule of Doc Holliday, the infamy of Billy the Kid. Then he laid the pistol aside and again lamented, "But, alas, the pistol is not the most dangerous weapon in the world."

Finally, from the sack, he drew out a huge cow's tongue which he had purchased from a local butcher. The tongue was ghastly, like a movie prop from *Friday the Thirteenth*. People drew away from its horror. "Here," he said, "is the most dangerous weapon in the world. Now open your Bibles to James 3." We did and he read to us point blank of the most dangerous weapon in the world. At the precise moment he drew the tongue from the bag, the "apocalypse" or "unveiling" ended. The tension he had created, with the drama of promise, was gone.

The apocalypse method of holding an audience in tension may also be used in combination with story forms. The story in and of itself may create tension, but the story itself may also exist to pull the cord. This draws the drape revealing the sermon theme. Such stories used in connection with this apocalypse method will generally be used at the first of the sermon.

The most dramatic use of this form of unveiling that I have ever seen was when my friend, Wendell Belew, preached a sermon called, "The Last Rock Uncle Billy Ever Sat On." In this sermon, Dr. Belew told of old Billy who went out with his mule one day to plow. The weather was incredibly hot. Uncle Billy, feeling the sweat pour off himself, stopped beneath the shade of an old oak tree to rest a minute. He found a huge rock, sat down on it; then he clutched his chest most suddenly and died. When Uncle Billy didn't come in for supper, Zeke went out looking for him. As dusk was gathering, Zeke found Uncle Billy. He had been dead for some time. The mule was still standing there swinging his ropy tail at petulant flies. The reins were wrapped around the plow handle just as the dead plowman had left them. Uncle Billy was lying on the ground.

Zeke was overcome with the stillness of the night. As he looked around and saw the mule, he said in muted grief, "Well, this is the last mule old Uncle Billy will ever hook a plow to. Yep!" he went on, "this is the last plow-handle Uncle Billy will ever guide around a field." He shaded his eyes against the setting sun and said, "This is the last furrow old Uncle Billy will ever turn." Looking at the old field boulder where Uncle Billy died, he rhapsodized, "This is the last rock Uncle Billy ever sat on."

Old Zeke left Uncle Billy's funeral services early and went back to the field. He found the "last rock Uncle Billy ever sat on." He picked and dug around the old boulder till finally it came free. He hooked a cable around it and had the old mule drag it home. But what's to be done with a rock that is forever in the way? Old Zeke put it right inside the front room door and he used it as a prop. Many who came to call asked old Zeke why he kept that big rock in the parlor. Tears would always come to his eyes and he would always tell the story of Uncle Billy. He would always end the story by saying, "And this, my friend, is the last rock Uncle Billy ever sat on." After years of repeating the story, old Zeke came home late one Saturday night from a barn dance. Being half-drunk, he stumbled into his home. In the dark, he tripped over the last rock Uncle Billy ever sat on, broke his neck, and died. Following this absorbing story, Dr. Belew showed us that the story was itself a drawing of the veil so he could reveal the main thesis of the sermon. He then delivered a powerful discourse on how contemporary churches stumble over the traditions of yesterday and destroy all hope of future vitality.

Transparency of Personhood. Personal transparency can serve to build tension. Confessional preaching is the medium. The process of the confession moves toward the key element we are set to reveal. Until the key element is revealed, the transparency continues to unfold itself. The confession will hold interest until it is told. Then the sermon will cease to hold interest.

It is said that when James Stewart, the great Scottish preacher, had been several weeks in his new parish, he was awakened at 4:00 A.M. one morning by the sound of traffic in the street in front of the parsonage. He looked out the window to see members of his parish going to work. They had been doing it every morning only he had not heard them before. His confession of this was a revelation, an unveiling of his own penance. He had slept while the men of his parish went off to work in the mines.

The ultimate revelation of his confession was that never more would his windows be dark while the men of the parish passed by. He kept his pledge.

Transparency of this sort made his sermons more credible.

In a much more contemporary view, I mentioned earlier the confessional sermon of fallen evangelist Jimmy Swaggart. I think it was the only sermon of his I ever listened to. In that sermon he voiced the utter transparency that catches the heart. Confession may always be a gentle but powerful lure for human attention.

Prophecy to Apocalypse. The best thing that can be said of drawing the curtain is that it is a powerful form of the inductive style. Revealing the sermon's agenda calls for the listeners to make their own decisions, to arrive at their own conclusions. The point communicated is left totally up to the hearer to interpret and apply.

Resolution: *Finis Benedictus*

The happy ending is not necessarily the best end for every sermon, but it is a sermon ending consistent with the message of the cross and empty tomb. Richard Lischer, in his *Theology of Preaching*, reminds us that the glorious theology of the sermon as a prime communication form is rooted in the never diminished hope that starts at the center of Christianity. This is anchored in the resurrection cry *Christus Resurrexit.* Every part of Christian theology and especially the sermon's theology is gathered beneath the cry, "He is risen!"

Theology in our hopeless day should focus on this doctrine of hope. Practically, *Christus Resurrexit* becomes the powerful fuel that drives the sermon.

When the tension of the sermon ends, it ought to end at the outcome of hope. Every sermon, like every act of ministry in the church, is to end this way.

As a pastor, I once entered into the I.C.U. of a hospital where a member of our church was dying. Accompanying me was one of the younger staff members of our church. The woman we were ministering to was so sick that her family had been called in. She would not live through the night, her doctor said. As we entered her room we prayed for her. I asked God to "heal her" and, after we prayed, we left the room. I sensed that the younger minister who had gone in with me to pray was uncomfortable with my prayer for her healing. After all, the woman was desperately ill. I tried to understand his feelings and wondered if I had prayed unrealistically in such a desperate setting. Still, hope is really the only merchandise of Christianity. Hope indeed is our treasure. It is a treasure that is kept in the interior storehouse of Christ's empty tomb.

The woman did live through the night. Within a few days an eighteen-year-old man, killed in a car accident in Tulsa, became her glorious donor. She received a new heart. She walked out of the hospital a week later. Again and again, I am reminded that desperation keeps no company with New Testament theology. The living Christ does!

Apply this truth to sermon preparation. Joy and victory are to set the tone of worship. Even more than this, joy and victory are to accompany almost every sermon. Even if the sermon has some non-joyous task to accomplish, these qualities should, at least, mark the sermon's overall tone. Certainly they should be there at the sermon's end.

Happy Ending—Tolkien's Challenge

In his *Essay on Faerie*, J. R. R. Tolkien deals with those final fairy-tale words, "and they lived happily ever after." These words could originate only in Christian lands. This is so because the ultimate hope represented by those words are attached to the Easter message *Christus Resurrexit*. The story of Jesus on Maundy Thursday and Good Friday is a woeful and debilitating tale, but on Easter morning the whole tale is revised. Joy reigns. This resultant ecstasy builds an inherent reign of joy within the believer's life. This treasure is dispersed in the preaching of the church.

This past year in the church I serve, a man stood at the front of the service just as the choir entered to begin worship. He clutched at his collar. Loosening his tie, he fell to the carpet, apparently dead. And about two thousand people watched for the next twenty-five minutes as doctors and nurses huddled over him and tried to save him. The rescue squad soon arrived. Again the same two thousand people looked on as the poor man was carried out on a gurney, his grieving wife following along behind. Throughout the confusion of this very visible passing (the man was officially pronounced dead by the end of the day), it fell my lot to preach. The sermon I had prepared to preach was a text from Acts 5 on the judgment of Ananias and Sapphira. Obviously, the text was inappropriate. I turned my text to the Book of Job, "My days are swifter than a weaver's shuttle" (Job 7:6).

It was not a genius's response to the crisis at hand. Still I made up my mind to preach not on the crisis but on the Christ. As I preached, I led the congregation in the mind's eye into the empty tomb and there we rejoiced with the only joy that might be had. Further, it seemed to me that our brother had died in the company of saints below to enter the company of saints above. In the midst of this argument, we were allowed to sorrow but not as those who have no hope (see 1 Thess. 4:13). The happy ending is the mandatory conclusion of those who walk with Christ in their hearts. It is to celebrate the indwelling Christ. It is to gild the mightiest treasure of the faith: the rich, empty tomb. Christ's empty grave flowers above every sadness with the joyous promise *Christus Resurrexit*. As Tolkien would have it, "we all lived happily ever after."

But aren't there times when the happy ending just doesn't apply? No, there are none; it always applies. Well, then aren't there times when it just doesn't fit? Perhaps. There is a kind of Christian extremism that is hyper-happy over heaven and a bit out of place when people genuinely grieve. C. S. Lewis's *A Grief Observed* is in many ways my least favorite of his books. This is probably so because I am unable to fit his desperation over the passing of his wife together with that utter confidence in Christ that he exhibits in the rest of his writings. This fault seems to be mostly mine. Nonetheless, *A Grief Observed* does sound a caution. At times our grief is so heavy that ultra-happiness cannot minister. Our need is too great. Giddy Christian joy at such moments seems unfeeling and non-empathetic.

The Post-Sermonic Mood

Not a great deal needs to be said about this subject. It is a commonly held theory that the kind of church to go to is the church you feel "good after." Of course, this is not a fetish of approval. Every sermon is not called to make people happy. Some are called to stir people to the point of examining who they are. Some are called to challenge them to the hard work of becoming what they ought to be. I remember in my early years standing strongly against the definitions of sin offered by the new morality scholars. "Morality is what you feel good after and immorality is what you feel bad after," they said. I certainly will not reduce sermons or worship to the status of happiness placebos. Still, a steady diet of sermons that you "feel bad after" cannot have much of heaven about them. Further, such sermons will also not attract a growing crowd of hearers. Their condemning and abusive themes hold little warmth. All things being equal, however, worship ought to leave a "smile in the heart and a spring in the step."

The movie or the Broadway play which leaves us in a state of buoyancy does perform a kind of service. Churches, like buoyant Broadway plays, can send people from the services with a touch of joy in their lives. Souls may exit churches humming or whistling a hymn. Such a mood-making service is also a friend-making service for the church. Euphoria is the best end for those who are willing to purchase their joy with their attention. Sermonic attention is the currency of this purchase. Those who listen with all their hearts leave worship taking its music with them into the world.

That final joy should be packaged in the heart. It should be carried out into the same hassled world that created the need for worship in the first place. In the utter heaviness of day-to-day living, the happy ending is a rich ministry. Preachers could learn from corporate motivators at this point. Positivist, motivational speakers give to their audience a euphoria that leaves all would-be entrepreneurs feeling good about the world and their place in it. The excessive fees that people pay to attend motivational conferences should serve as instruction to sermon writers. People want to give their attention. They want to believe that when the preacher releases their attention, he or she will send them back into the world feeling good about who they are.

The Resolution Triptych

The best kind of sermonizing will move through three separate and definable stages—tension, decision, and peace. A sermon should reach the acme of perfection. It will then be so relevant with content that it will set up a riveting disequilibrium.

The call of such disequilibrium will be decision. The point and logic of the sermon will then be served. They will ask all those who attend our words to make some decision. Once they do decide, their attention should be rewarded with resolution. The best possible resolution to tension is release. The best kind of release will send the congregation out into the world with a feeling of rightness about who they are and what God has called them to do.

Key Five:

Constructing a Pyramid of Priorities

Time's glory is to calm contending kings,
To unmask falsehood and bring truth to light,
To stamp the seal of time in aged things,
To wake the morn and sentinel the night,
To wrong the wronger till he render right.[43]

The Audience Challenge of

Key Five

Dear Speaker:

The world has never gotten over its likin' of the truth. I've been a member of a church now for more'n fifty years. We must have had twenty pastors or more. I don't know for sure. None of 'em stayed very long. Everyone of them told the truth. In fact they could bore you for hours on end with the truth. There was only one out of the whole bunch that we ever really wanted to keep. He told the truth interestingly. One time he put on his bathrobe and played like he was King David. Sure was interesting. Another time he played like he was the innkeeper in Bethlehem. Then one time he smeared his face with soot—sure looked strange—and told us he was Job. We all knew better and he knew we did, but I never really understood the Book of Job till that sermon. One time he dressed up in a white robe and came in the back of the auditorium carrying a sign. He told us he was an Archangel. He seemed so convinced, we believed him. Darndest thing, he'd do per't near't anything to keep our attention. He always did. Big church down in Chattanooga hired him away from us. The good 'uns always seem to get away.

They arrested a man over by Greenville the other day. They threw him in jail. He was walking around town in a white robe, carrying a sign that said "THE WORLD IS COMING TO AN END." I don't know why they arrested him. Most everybody believed he was right. As I saw it, he was telling the truth interestingly. Last week my preacher preached on that very thing. The way he told that same truth wasn't all that interesting. They might have locked up the wrong man.

It sure seems important to me to tell the truth interestingly. Not too many people do it. A bunch of us who listen to your sermons are wishing you'd do it. You might try the white robe and sign routine. Just don't go outside.

—Your Audience

A Key Five communicator should be concerned with three priorities—truth, interest, and inspiration. I have listed these three values in their proper order. They are pyramidal in the sense that each is foundational to its successor. For instance, until we have made sure that we are telling the truth, it is immoral to try to interest them in what we are saying. If we communicate the truth and do not interest our listeners, we may be vital but boring. Until we have told the truth in such a way as to interest them, inspiration will be missing. Inspiration cannot issue from pedestrian truth.

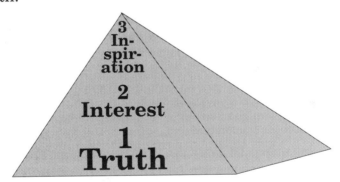

3 In-spir-ation

2 Interest

1 Truth

THE COMMUNICATOR'S PYRAMID OF PRIORITIES

Developing the Pyramid

What is the preacher's responsibility in developing this pyramid of communication? The values in the pyramid do not spring automatically into our sermons as we deliver them; rather, they come from disciplined preparation. None of these values have to do with the personality of the speaker. They have nothing to do with the personality of the audience.

Serving this pyramid of values has to do with five items. The first is the preacher's grasp of the information to be communicated in the speech. A second item has to do with the preacher's word choice. Third, an ability to use good dynamics in delivery is also critical. Fourth, every sermonizer needs a sense of venture. This daring will allow for the courage to say all that needs to be said to get the point across. Finally, the communicator must have a honed sensitivity to the audience. All these elements of audience concern will confer interest upon the sermon. And best of all, the content will never arrive faster than they can grasp it.

THE 5 SERVANTS OF THE PYRAMID OF VALUES

1 The Speaker's Grasp of Content

2 Oratorical Polish

3 The Use of Communicative Dynamics

4 The Speaker's Courage to Inform

5 The Speaker's Audience-Sensitivity

Preparation

For any preacher to offer content, there is but one word which is all-important: *preparation*. In securing basic pyramidal truth, only preparation will serve. While truth is entirely a matter of integrity, we must study it to be sure that our grasp of it is in place. Further, we must study to make it interesting. We must study to find ways to keep truth simple—to make sure our hearers find it reachable.

It is a rare thing to find a speaker firmly in charge of his subject. But it is easy to find preachers who present strong truths weakly. Every time I hear one do it, I ask myself, "What went wrong with the preparation?" What caused the preacher to ignore the study needed to convince the audience that the truth being spoken was significant? Should the speaker have stayed in the study longer? Could more statistics have been garnered to convince us that this was the most important truth in the world? Could the delivery have buttressed the argument with a heavy quote by someone of great renown? How could the preachers present the truth to make it seem "even truer"?

Whatever the answers are, they all have to do with preparation. The longer the communicator stays in the study, mulling the "stuff" of the speech in the mind, the more credible the truth will appear in the delivery. Fred Craddock reminds us:

> Study is a homiletical act: the confidence-born of study (not the pseudo-confidence of personality or bravado) releases the powers of communication. To know one's subject and to believe it is important, is to be free, and it is freedom that permits all one's faculties to have their finest hour in the service of speaking and hearing.[44]

Any sermon worth doing well proceeds from a fully developed communication brief. If the sermon is critically important, a complete manuscript should be developed. Why? Because a fully developed document best conveys the argument of the communiqué. Crafting the sermon makes sure that the content is worthy of listener attention. Only as we have a fully prepared document can we inspect the argument and judge whether it is really worthy.

Robert Hughes said that without criticism there is no art. Sermonic art like any other cannot exist without it. Practically speaking, only a full manuscript gives us a chance to polish sermon phraseology. Likewise, the dynamics of our delivery cannot be planned or rehearsed until we have a full document in hand.

We have all heard the stories of theatrical preachers who, in preparing their sermons, wrote in the margins their melodramatic emphases: "Cry here! Pound the pulpit, here! Drop to your knees and sing 'Mother's Bible,' here!" As ludicrous as this sounds, such annotated manuscripts allow the speaker to plan the dynamics of delivery.

Oratorical Improvement

Now let us examine the issue of dynamics. Preaching well is not just an understanding of what we are going to say, but how we are going to say it. Although chapter 7 will discuss rehearsing the sermon, let's look at the relationship between the rehearsal and the practice of dynamics. Before a sermon can even be rehearsed, its state of preparation must be complete. Then the preacher can see what those dynamics are just by looking at the manuscript. The communicator may actually write in the margins of the manuscript some specific instructions of how something is to be said. I might, for instance, write in the margin, "Step out from behind the pulpit and quote this poem," or I might write, "Use a pompous theatrical tone, [as I did in communicating the voice of the Pharisee in my sermon, The Needy Publican]."

Recently I quoted Yoda of the *Star Wars* films. Next to the quote, I wrote, "Use actual dialect here!" In using this quote I knew that the dialect was not necessary. Usually, it is unwise to use geographical dialect in our multicultural world. But in some few cases, if done well, it can render a sermon more interesting. Nothing, however, should be done from the pulpit that might suggest bigotry.

Venture

The sermon is under obligations to tell the truth. But it must tell the truth with a spirit of venture. Great truths can rarely be told without some risk. Sometimes the truth will be so gangling as to cause the audience to doubt the thesis. At other times, the truth is so critical that it may only be told at great personal risk to the preacher's reputation.

In dealing with other difficult truths, some risk may arise in the area of audience receptivity. Often, it takes a great deal of courage to tell the most important truths. In a day when political correctness has become common, to speak any of our deep convictions may anger someone. In this impatient generation, some listeners will no longer give attendance to things they do not believe. Such audiences are quick to put feet to their hang-ups and walk out. While we will deal with such antagonisms in chapter 6, let it be said here that the preacher's kindness must accompany courage.

How are preachers to react when people grow angry and leave a service? In the Gospels, Jesus lectured on being "the bread come down from heaven!" This truth was so offensive that many "walked away." Jesus seems not to rebuke their going, but He does ask His disciples, "Will ye also go away (John 6:67)?" Peter replied by asking, "Lord, to whom shall we go? You have the words of eternal life [the truth]." Jesus further warned in the Beatitudes that they were the most blessed who had all manner of things said against them falsely and yet remained true to their Father in heaven (see Matt. 5:11). Paul said that the time would come when men would not endure doctrine, but heap to themselves teachers who entertained them but never told them the entire truth (see 2 Tim. 4:3).

David Buttrick said that popular rejection may not come from their disbelief but from their unwillingness to accept the truth because of what it requires:

> Preaching may also be met with what the Bible terms "hardness of heart." No matter how winsome in style or generous in promise, preaching can be met with fierce opposition. People may oppose the goodness because they have overinvested in "this present age." They are afraid they will lose what they have, power, possession or prestige.[45]

Our own times have a kind of multicultural and unkind aura about them. On many college campuses now, I find my interest in the truth scoffed at or at least rudely ignored. Students and adults alike noisily walk out of assemblies they wish to protest. But this kind of behavior demands that those who feel compelled to preach the truth should determine to do it persuasively. They should be as prepared as possible. Most of all, they should determine to be as kind as possible in extending, even to hecklers, a Christlike courtesy. Christian communicators serve the One whose courteous but unflagging commitment to His righteousness forgave all antagonists from His cross. Those who preach the whole counsel of God are part of Christ's glorious "fellowship of suffering" (Phil. 3:10).

Our preaching of truth must proceed from an undaunted spirit of venture. Every audience will contain those who come willingly to hear us. Once there, however, they may decide that they strongly disagree. The days are gone when they would have sat till the sermon was over. Now they stand and walk out to register their disagreement. Sometimes they remain seated and do it all with body language. To love truth means that we are already defending with courage the most basic level of our pyramid of values.

Audience Sensitivity

Whether we are able to start with truth and move the audience through interest to inspiration will depend on these four factors: audience analysis, the pacing of information, the quantity of information, and finally, creative rapport.

The preacher's sensitivity to the audience will require him or her to operate on two mental frequencies. One of those circuits will be turned to delivery; the other part of the mind will turned to the frequency of feed-back. The sermon's monitoring track continually gives instructions to the delivery mechanism. It

THE FOUR VALUES OF AUDIENCE SENSITIVITY

✳ ANALYSIS

✳ PACING

✳ QUANTITY OF DATA

✳ CREATIVE RAPPORT

says, "slow down, speed up, say something funny—they're drifting." It may say "jump ahead to your next more interesting point; draw this story out—they are really into this one." The interplay of these two tracks working together says that you are not merely speaking, you are "communicating." More than that, you are actually speaking to the audience, for their sake. The monitoring track of the mind during delivery says that the preacher sees the audience as worthy people. He or she will not leave them in the dark, unattended.

The monitoring track shows the speaker's sensitivity. It communicates that every blink of your eye, every movement of your body is important. Each tells me how you feel. I will not proceed without adjusting my speech to your comprehension. When I can, I will adjust my speech to meet what your body language tells me is your philosophy. Where my truth is not adjustable, I will come as far as I can to meet your viewpoint.

Strong and Cook wisely counsel: "The more you know about your audience, the greater are your chances of achieving your persuasive goals. Over and

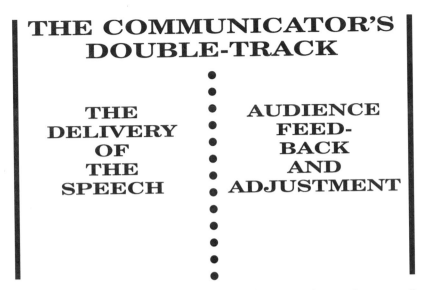

THE COMMUNICATOR'S DOUBLE-TRACK

| THE DELIVERY OF THE SPEECH | AUDIENCE FEED-BACK AND ADJUSTMENT |

over during the research and preparation phases of your speech you should ask the question, 'Who is my audience?'"[46]

This kind of audience analysis is a computerized scanning of the audience by the speaker's mind. It registers such things as age group, gender, socioeconomic background, educational levels, etc. This kind of processing tells the preacher how he or she must pace the argument being presented. Once the audience analysis is complete, the communicator will have already set the pace at which the audience can best receive the communiqué. For instance a talk on the H.I.V. virus will move at one pace for single adults, another pace for a medical convention, and quite another pace for a junior high school health class. In preaching, for instance, biblical exegesis can fly faster at the Sunday night assembly than it can with the Sunday morning crowd. Audience analysis should dictate the pace.

Even if we have properly analyzed our audience, we will still have to depend on the monitoring track of our minds. It will tell us when we are moving at just the right pace. If there is any doubt as to whether we are going too fast or too slow, faster is probably the better fault. Faster will at least teach them more, not less, than they bargain for; thus, they will see it as a better use of their time. When we underpace a piece, we do not challenge our audience to reach.

I think teaching them to reach is especially important in a local pastorate. It is also critical when you are delivering a whole series of sermons to the same congregation. It is generally better to have audiences wishing you wouldn't go so fast than to leave them hoping you'll "get on with it." A dawdling delivery allows their minds to frolic in fields afar. They will roam in distant mental grottoes till you come back to them with the next scrap of information they want to appropriate.

A few years ago I preached in a rural Kansas church. My audience analysis before the sermon began told me that these people were definitely not "bumpkins." Still, their knowledge of Cicero and the Cartesian cogito was underdeveloped. I, therefore, cut way back on the pacing. Yet after the fourth of my five-sermon series, one dear sister said to me, rather pointedly, "My dear Dr. Miller, I can't understand a thing you say." While her body language had been telling me this during my three earlier sermons, her remarks still hurt.

I thought about her rejoinder for a moment and said, "I am very sorry about this. I'll certainly try to do better." Then I added as kindly as I could manage, "Maybe God wanted us to meet in this church, so that I could learn to stoop a little and you could learn to reach."

Whether or not I should have made such a comment I'm not sure. But I am sure of this: stooping is always good for a speaker to do. Reaching , likewise, should always be the posture of the audience. My game of rac-quetball is less than Olympic, but I have noticed that it only improves when I play people who are better than I am. Reaching is the way that I improve my game. Similarly, when I pay money to attend a semi-nar, I do so because I want to listen to people who know more than I do. Most people only attend church-es where they see the preacher as more competent in understanding the Bible than they themselves are. Congregational pacing assumes that the preacher can and should run biblically faster than the congregation does.

Discriminating audiences always demand content. The quality of that content must give evidence that the speaker has spent worthy time in preparation. The preparation becomes obvious when the sermon pace keeps them reaching. Further the preacher's handling of the information will make the delivery rare and commanding.

When all is said and done, your sensitivity to your audience means that you want to merge with your audience. You want to feel a commonality of moods. You want to be one with them in joy, laughter, grief, pain, etc. Still, you want quality content. You want to say it better, prettier, artsier, and far more creative than they have ever heard it before. You want them to feel a variety of moods within a framework of ensnar-ing creativity. You want them to confess after your ser-mon that while they may have heard the things you're saying, they have never heard them said in that way.

Creative rapport, therefore, is not just being one with an audience. It is a creative oneness that indi-cates you are intriguing them with sermon crafting, word management, and the control of your unique presentation. This creative energy locks you and your listeners in a bonding of compulsion. As they begin to feel this creative rapport, you wield a powerful scepter from atop the communication pyramid.

As we begin to examine the base of the pyramid—truth—it might be good to remind yourself that creative rapport and doctrine should walk together. Truth in the church, especially doctrinal truth, is rarely seen by those who attend a church as being light on its feet. In fact, truth—divorced from this creative rapport—is usually a plodding. Much to be desired is that preacher who can touch truth with creativity. Truth appears beautiful on the lips of those who really know how to communicate it.

At this point in considering audience rapport we need to remember the Aristotelian communication triad: *ethos, logos,* and *pathos.* The *ethos* (or deportment and motive) of the speaker must be sterling in intention. Then he or she will be able to speak a *logos* (or message) that is worthy to be heard and acted upon. Finally, when both *ethos* and *logos* are in place the *pathos* (or rapport) of audience and speaker will be one.

If the speaker's *ethos* is corrupt, then the *logos* will be self-seeking and the *pathos* of the audience will render them feeling tricked or deceived. If the speaker's *ethos* is sterling but the *logos* is not well developed, the *pathos* will be rendered suspect. If any portion of the Aristotelian triad is weak or incorrect, the communiqué will be spoiled. How often we hear of shysters who nonetheless preach a true gospel. The *ethos* is wrong but the *logos* is correct. Even so the *pathos* of the audience is justly suspicious.

THE ARISTOTELIAN TRIAD

Truth

According to Jesus, of all the components of speech, only truth liberates. Jesus never said, "You shall learn the art of illustration and the illustration will set you free." Nor did He ever say, "Go ye into all the world and craft your communication." There is only one primary commodity for the kingdom of God and that is truth. All sermons, whether preached to a small congregation or the Rose Bowl, will only be measured at that final tribunal on the basis of their integrity.

For a moment, let us equate theology and truth. Indeed, theology and truth are one. Theology originated in sermons. It did not spring from books first. In every sense it must be admitted that faith created theology; theology did not create faith. In other words, people first believed. As they wrote down what they believed, theology came to be. Since Jesus and His disciples were the first to articulate what they believed, they actually created New Testament theology. Any communication that ignores theological truth is not Christian communication.

A Key Five Christian communicator understands that the integrity of a speech and the theological precision of it are exactly the same thing. It angers me when I hear a person make a moving speech whose *ethos* is flawed with poor theology. A certain pastor of my acquaintance was a remarkable speaker and well loved by his growing and prestigious congregation. But on one occasion, after a member of the church committed suicide, he preached a very moving sermon on why suicides go to heaven. Suicides have to go to heaven, he said, because there is no hell.

It was a powerful and well crafted sermon. His logic consoled his congregation, but only with bad theology. Suicides, like those who die in other ways, go either to heaven or hell. But their destiny is dependent upon truth that is bound up in a theology of integrity. So if we apply Jesus' words to this sermon—"You shall know the truth, and the truth shall set you free"—those who attended that very moving sermon may still be captive. And in this case, the rhetoric that might have liberated them was flawed.

Inauthentic sermons do not always originate in an intentional deception. We can give our audience the impression that we are telling insignificant truth by clowning in the pulpit. Eloquence like humor can hold an audience with riveted attention. Still, the riveting may cause the audience to believe it is hearing the truth when actually it may be deceived by a slick presentation.

Augustine said,

> Always beware, however, of the man who

abounds in eloquent nonsense, especially if the hearer is pleased with worthless oratory and thinks that because the speaker is eloquent what he says must be true. As that great teacher of rhetoric, Cicero, rightly said, "Although wisdom without eloquence is often of little service, eloquence without wisdom does positive injury, and is never of service."[47]

We who preach are responsible for telling the truth. At the risk of being redundant let me say it again: we cannot all be orators of note, but we can all tell the truth. Let us therefore examine the truth for which we are responsible.

Truth as Fact

There is no more honest statement of truth than the creeds of the church. But there is one truth more ordinal: the Bible. It is for this reason that the Bible is the basis of sermons. It is for that reason that the Bible is read as a part of the sermon. If the facts of the sermon do not match the facts of the Bible, then we have sinned against the pyramidal priority of truth.

The first way to violate this priority is to overtly take a position by saying something like, "While the Bible says such and such, I will shortly tell you what the Bible really means by what it is saying." Often such statements are preface to a deviation of some sort. Some might say, "While the apostle said this in good faith, many things have changed since he said this. . . ." Or "Had Jesus lived in our day, he would have said. . . ." Or "The point is not so much to tell you what Hosea said, but what he meant by what he said. . . ." It seems to me that much error begins in just such prefaces. From Marcion to Bishop Pike, a lot of error has been preached in the kinder name of helping people "really" understand what the truth is for their day.

But there is another devious way around telling the truth. It is a kind of preaching which ignores the text. So often today I hear someone preach the Bible, and yet when they get through, I can find no obvious connection between the text they read and the sermon they preached. This is a kind of lie. It is not blatant, nor is it mean. But it is false, for it generally carries the impression that we have heard the Bible preached, when in truth we have not. Preaching the Bible is taking a text, reading it, and letting God speak through it to the people. The non-textual sermon steals God's voice, supplanting it with weaker information, and anemic authority.

Truth as Experience

But assuming that the text and the discourse have joined to tell the truth, how do we make the truth usable? We illustrate it, craft it, and make it interesting. Best of all, we set it within the matrix of our experience. Truth then becomes usable. Every time the communicator says, "Here's how this truth became usable to me," the audience moves closer. At such words their minds register the word *relevant*. Relevance is, after all, usable truth.

There is a very old story about a man who lectured at great length on pelicans. The congregation responded, "Actually he told us more about pelicans than we really wanted to know." The real objection was that he gave out unusable truth. I once read about a lunatic in Tokyo who wandered the streets crying, "The world is round like an orange! The world is round like an orange!" He was locked up, not for telling a lie, but for telling truth that didn't matter.

It is not only important to preach the Bible but to preach it in relevant ways. To preach the ethnic importance of the table of nations will not generally hold the same mesmerizing power as preaching the third chapter of John. Eschatology is a nice speculative subject for a "deeper life group" on Thursday night, but few baby boomers I know are drawn to church just dying to find out what the third toe of the great beast of Revelation really represents. Usable, experience-tested truth is the business of the sermonizer.

Truth as Transference

The on-line communicator announces with energetic body language, if in no other way, "My truth is usable! Here's how I can transfer its implications to your life." Transference is really a psychological process in which the feelings of the counselee are transferred to the therapist. But in this sense I like thinking of it as the truth of Scripture in the life experience of the communicator which gets transferred to the life of the listener.

In homiletics, this is called application. It is that step of the sermon by which truth is joined to the personal belief system of those who attend the sermon. It is a mistake to see the sermon as finished until this occurs. If there is no application, there is no sermon.

Interest

The heavy burden of supplying interest to the church service is not the job of the sermon alone. Worship itself must supply much of the interest. While that subject belongs to another book, let us briefly say that worship, like sermons, can be either interesting or dull. It is indeed a rare church where the same good adjective modifies both. But if the worship is creative, original, spontaneous, and alive, the sermon has a much better chance of being all those things as well. In our pyramid of communication values, it is the truth which changes us, but it is interest that entices us to listen to the truth. Exactly how does interest entice us? By what I like to call the three "Let Me's" of audience interest.

Let Me Entertain You

Entertainment and interest pass very close. It is difficult to tell if a sermon has interested or entertained the audience. Craig Loscalzo says the categories do not have to be separate: "People do not, or at least should not, come to church to be entertained; yet that doesn't mean that what they hear in our sermons need not be interesting. People pay attention when what they hear is interesting to them, when they sense that the sermon has import for their lives."[48]

I also want to make a case for not working too hard to separate these two values. We should never become a grandstander with a performer's need to be applauded. But in our entertainment age, people will welcome a bit of light-hearted logic that keeps them laughing, or at least smiling, as they learn.

Therefore, this first "let me" is not meant to be cheap or bawdy in lieu of the high work of the sermon. Still, it calls the sermon to be creative when it asks hundreds, if not thousands, of people for their attention. Without some entertaining, the sermon will have a harder time getting the attention of those to whom it wishes to give the life-changing truth it holds.

But the entertainment aspect of the sermon will not come as easy for some as it does for others. In fact, for many the dimension will be all but impossible. I would suggest that while the entertainment attempt will include humor and story, it is composed of serious elements as well. Things like testimony and story may not be inherently funny, but they may hold a riveting rapport with the audience.

In some sense then, I believe that all can experiment with how to hold an audience's attention. To entertain means to occupy their time engagingly. Every time I am prone to doubt the value of this engagement, I turn again to the arts for the best demonstration of this. Movies, plays, novels, paintings all have the same glorious virtue: the arts intrigue us as they teach us.

Not only do the arts teach us entertainingly, they also have for their most descriptive word *creative*. To pull that word into the preparation and delivery of sermons is the most grueling of considerations. For creativity is an awesome task. It is this effort that makes us pore over our communiqué by asking if we have said it in the strongest possible way. It asks also if we have illustrated it with the best possible material. Creativity stirs the deepest levels of our experience to draw from those depths that will give our sermons high intrigue. We "desire creativity, for without it the sermon barrel empties and the minds in the pews switch to pause."[49] As is the effort, so also the reward.

Creative anythings are hard to come by and always in demand. Certainly this is true of preachers.

Let Me Instruct You

The first "let me" can come across as "cute." This "let me" may come across as arrogant. If we become too obvious in our desire to instruct our listeners, we may seem conceited. The whole idea is to communicate subtly. Again, remember that most are sitting in attendance because they believe that your stream of experience is larger than theirs. They expect you to instruct them. They are quite willing to "let you" do so. But never injure their dignity by insulting their "immature level" of experience. Never make over your own intelligence to the extent that you denigrate their personhood.

Let Me Help You to Apply This Truth

This "let me" holds some possibility of implied arrogance, but it is generally a wonderful and welcome part of any communication. Everybody welcomes genuine help and they will be most enthused about yours.

Inspiration

This is the highest level in the pyramid and the least reachable for most communicators. But after we have told the truth, and done so interestingly, we must move to this final glorious level of communication. This ultimate plateau is reached when the hard work of creative preparation combines with the preacher's natural passion. Where these two things meet, inspiration is born. Let us see if we can answer these three questions: First, "Why should your moods borrow from mine?" The second question is "Why should you be so intensely involved in the issues of this sermon?" The final question, having to do with inspiration is, "Why you have no choice but to decide this? Do it now! It is a matter of supreme conscience."

Why Should Your Moods Borrow from Mine?

This question will only arise occasionally in a speech if the speaker is truly inspirational. What indicates the presence of inspiration in a sermon? Generally the homily will be so buoyant that the audience will lose track of objectivity. Why should the listener's mood be the same as that of the speaker's? The very question is too academic to surface in the sea of subjective emotion that the sermon is creating. The speaker is excited. Every fiber of sermonic passion is electric so they dare not fail to listen, and to act.

The strength of passion makes them concerned about the preacher's issue. But when passion is coupled to creative delivery, most questions of logic are academic. Subconsciously the listener is afire, "My intensity is the same as the preacher's. The world's afire! Can't you see there is no other way to feel about it?"

Why Should You Be Intensely Involved?

This question is rather related to the previous one. The only real answer has to do with contagion. Contagion is the pathology of interest. It shouts that inspiration is more "caught than taught." During moments of inspiration, there is little use in asking why we are involved; it is as pointless as asking someone why he has the flu. The only answer is, "I caught it!"

Intense involvement is generally a group infection. It is so tightly communicative that the only way to escape the contagion is quarantine. Most of us under the passionate spell of inspiration are so gloriously one that we have no choice but to yield to the unifying force that sweeps us into the propositions of the preacher. Our involvement then not only begins as a voluntary offering, it ends in a mandate to pay attention. That mandate does not come from the preacher but from ourselves. We slap our own sluggishness across the chops. We say, "Get out of your day dreams. An issue of grave importance is being described. You are involved. If you fail to listen, a significant part of your future and self-development will be amputated. Wake every gland. Expose every nerve end! Rebuke all your sluggish senses! Join the army of the enthralled! They are sitting all around you. They will act when you do."

Why Is Decision Your Only Choice?

Decision is the final and glorious end of inspiration. In the fury of the way that I feel about this, the time has come to make a decision. I will decide in joy! But the decision is never one forced by the communicator. The decision is one that grows out of the listeners intense, inescapable, involvement in the communiqué.

I have been a part of Baptist congregations all my life. I have asked again and again, "What is it that impels (or compels) people to come to the altar?" Of course, the Holy Spirit cannot be left out of the recipe.

But in short, inspired people decide; uninspired people do not. Again the recipe is simple. Developing a good manuscript or communication brief comes first. Editing that manuscript or brief into a creative document is step two. Step three comes when we begin to involve ourselves in our subject. This mystique furnishes us with a passion that reaches out to include others in our involvement. Step four occurs when the audience, who at first only appreciates our enthusiasm, comes to identify with it and then finally embraces it.

Key Five communicators take logical steps through the pyramid of communication values. In the movement from truth to inspiration, the power of the sermon is born. You will likely find the movement less one-two-three than I have described it. Becoming a great preacher, like becoming a great artist, requires a life commitment. Like an artist, such communicators move through their world, asking of all that they see and touch, "How am I to make use of what I am experiencing right now?"

Life is not here merely to house us. Life is a resource center that furnishes the content and passion of our homiletics. A flower, a child's prayer, an earthquake in Central America, a friend's funeral, a paragraph of a novel, the "stupid thing that happened in the supermarket," the kite that never flew, Hamlet's last words, the statistics you saw in *USA Today*: all are there for our use. With these samplings of life, we bless their knowledge with our experience. They become at first interested and then inspired. Properly challenged, they decide on a bold course of action. They act, not always because they want to, but because we have spoken with such compulsion we have made it impossible to do anything else.

Key Six:

Making Sure They Hear Through a Trinity of Audio Values

He was wont to speak plain and to the purpose like an honest man and a soldier, and now is he turned orthography, his words are a very fantastical banquet—just so many strange dishes. May I be so converted, and see with these eyes?[50]

The Audience Challenge
of
Key Six

Dear Speaker:

Nobody I know likes a monotone drone. I wish you preachers could see that the conversations which define our lives come at us with a variety of intensity. We shout. We whisper. We laugh, cry, yell, and remain silent. Why is it that sermons so often come at us in a voice that never varies in its intensity?

I'd listen better to sermons if everything you say didn't sound the same. You want my attention? Then don't talk about the crucifixion with the same, even voice you use to describe the wedding at Cana. Don't talk about the resurrection with the same voice you use to describe the kosher code of Leviticus.

We had a preacher some years ago that spoke so softly that you could hardly hear him. We had another that was really an adenoidal lungbuster. We always felt bad that we could never hear the first one. But we felt really bad that we could hear the second one.

But the worst case scenario is a monotone. We had one of those kind o' preachers too. We finally got a new public-address system, thinking it would help. But it didn't. Microphones can make a dull speech louder, but that's about it.

You know what I think? I think you preachers should be made to study drama . . . at gunpoint, if necessary. Actors—even the bad ones—seem to know how to make their voices serve all the emotions of life. When they grow angry and talk loud, we never seem to get a headache. Even when they whisper, we can always hear them. I wish preachers were more like actors. Then sermons would be as interesting as the theater.

—Your Audience

The electronic variables of every speaking engagement bring a nightmare of concern. The whole issue of audio systems causes our blood to freeze. Which of us has not barely survived a bad sound system? Which of us has not known the horrible shriek of feedback? It screams its head-splitting howls into the middle of our finest sermons.

It unnerves us to see the shiny, erect totem of a microphone stand. Haughty it stands. Its serpentine black wires wind like anorexic vipers around our feet. Which of us have not seen the microphone crook, beckoning like the finger of Lucifer, and begging us come to his sacrifice? Some amplifiers are doubtless assembled in hell by demons.

To be honest, I have little counsel on what do with the malfunctioning electronics of our trade. My only words of wisdom are two: first, pay very close attention when the technician is "wiring you for sound." Looking down at the nest of black wires twisting about your feet while you try to find the microphone switch usually embarrasses you later. Much of the agony we experience when being "wired for sound" is our fault. Sometimes our malaise comes because we get to the "wiring area" late. Consequently, in a hurried and confused state we meet the technician. Often the "mike man" is trying to "hook us up" and give us critical information as we are sticking out our hand to meet other platform people. In the middle of such activities, we have neglected to listen when we were told where the microphone switch was.

A second piece of advice I freely offer: Get to the

auditorium where you are to speak in time to hear the speaker before you (unless you are lamentably first on the program). By getting there at this early hour, you can watch and listen to your predecessor. Is she screaming to make up for what she feels the audio system isn't doing? Is he coping with a feedback problem? Is she kicking cords out of the way as she tries to deliver her message? If you notice him coping with a feedback problem even as he speaks, get to the sound board and talk to the sound engineer ahead of time. Tell the technician diplomatically that you want the problem eliminated. Never be ugly, but make it very clear that you would rather have no microphone system than to cope with a malfunction as the current speaker is doing. One other word of wisdom: don't be afraid of doing without the system at all. It is better to be heard poorly than to be interrupted by the ear-splitting screams of a bad system. Besides, communication can occur without them.

I used to wonder how Jesus, Paul, Whitefield, and Wesley ever addressed thousands without any amplification equipment. Then one night, while waiting my turn to speak at the Glorieta Conference Center in New Mexico, I discovered how they did it. My lesson came while I was waiting to speak to a crowd of some three thousand people in a huge auditorium. Outside a fierce electrical storm was raging. Intermittent bolts of lightning were causing the lights and the audio system to blink on and off. A dynamic contralto soloist preceded me. She was faced with a full-power microphone that came and went with every blinking of the lights. Ever and anon, an electrical surge would kill the lights and sound system. In the interim when there was no power, the magnificence of her voice would fade. When she was not booming her bombastic song, she was only a barely perceptible, quiet human voice, isolated and alone in the huge dark auditorium.

I never like to claim the power of prayer, especially in electronic matters. This probably amounts to a weakness in my theology, but I have always had this feeling that God also doesn't care much for electronics and rarely gets involved in microphone systems. Still I did pray on this occasion, "Lord, I don't mind having sound and I don't mind doing without it, but, if you don't mind, I'd like it one way or the other." Just as the sometimes-amplified-sometimes-not contralto was finishing her solo, everything went dead.

She and I shuffled past each other in the murk of the emergency lighting system as I walked to the completely dead microphone. Its spastic, on-again-off-again final gasps had just destroyed her solo. I knew all hell was doubled up in laughter because the woman's self-esteem must have been as dead as the amplifier. When I asked God to give me either microphone or no microphone, I had supposed that He would graciously give me full light and power. It would have made a nice prayer testimony in later sermons. Alas, He had chosen to answer in a way that was not entirely to my liking. But, at least, there were no power surges. Metaphorically, I have begun many a sermon in the dark and oft ended them there. But this darkness was more than symbolic.

I could not see the audience's faces as I stood before the deceased microphone. I even wondered if I should call off the meeting and tell everyone to go home. On the contrary, I decided to go on with the effort. So I shouted out over the sea of dark faces, "Can you hear me?" I thought, if no answer comes back, we'll all go home. My unamplified question sounded thin in the darkness. It seemed as if I could barely hear it. But to my amazement, a thin voice answered from somewhere far off in the gloom—perhaps from the back row—"Preach on, brother!" So I launched out on my sermon. I could not see my notes, which taught me a strange reliance on what I could dredge up from my preparation. I felt a further need to depend on God.

In a few moments as I "preached on," two men, armed with five-cell flashlights, came. They stood at the near edge of a balcony and shined their thin little lights upon me. It was an odd sensation. People sat quietly and listened. It amazed me that they would do it. There was no movement in the audience. They seemed somehow rapt, like enraptured early Christians on a midnight hilltop. My energy-efficient sermon moved on. Illuminated by the ghostly light of batteries, God seemed eerily close at hand. I got this feeling that for the first time in my ministry, people were hearing me—not boom-boxes, computer chips, and hot-wires—me. Here, *sans* power-plant assistance, people were hearing the gospel, just as they must have heard it in the time of Christ or the Reformers.

That night I learned that just as microphone systems may make it easy for people to hear, they also make it easy for people to get disinterested. When there is a microphone system in place, they can periodically leave the sermon always throbbing in the air around their disinterested souls. They can abandon it and return to it whenever they like. But without amplifiers they must do more work. They must participate in the work of communication or there will be none. So I repeat my lesson for your benefit: never fear the loss or absence of a system. Generally you can do without one.

The Use of Technology in Communication

The key is to use technology and not be mastered by it. Sound boards and technicians should function in such a way as to benefit, not enslave, you. If you find yourself on a very short lavaliere-microphone cord, and you like to roam wider than it allows you, ask for another that will set you free. If there is an ear-splitting feedback screech, ask the technicians to either shut off the screech or the microphone. If they refuse to do either, lay the microphone down and walk away from it. Be firm—like Jesus . . . somewhat. The key is to do it your way, not theirs. Beware when they ask you to use an old microphone so they can give the "good mike" to the "really great speaker" who is to follow or precede you. Remind them that you are also one of God's children, and that "all of God's children gotta have mikes!" Such requests are usually honored.

You should never argue with "the sound squad," since it is generally not possible to win an open confrontation. Do what you must do to be heard. Let technology and the technicians help you if they will. Do it the best way you can, if they will not. There is only one cardinal rule in this matter. If it comes down to pleasing either the sound squad or the audience, always favor the audience.

There are five basic steps which must be taken to deal with other audio-visual barriers to communication. The first has to do with lighting.

Lighting and Hearing: The Psychological Ears of the Eyes

Yes, you heard it right! People cannot hear well if

the lighting is poor. Light is the psychological ear that makes hearing possible. The two souls who may have made my non-electronic sermon work were probably the guys with the flashlights. What people can't see they will not attend well. Unfortunately, lighting is much harder to deal with on the spot than are the sound problems. Some buildings are so dark that seeing is impossible. Sometimes the theater people of a nearby college or community acting guild may be able to lend a temporary lighting system or spotlight. But often this is not possible to arrange on the spot. If the lecture is a part of a series, the first one may be the only one that is absolutely necessary to deliver in the dark. Following that introductory speech, some additional lighting can be brought in before the second lecture is to be delivered.

Whatever is done or not done, please remember that people must be able to see or they may lose interest. In especially large auditoriums, such as convention halls where thousands of people may be in attendance, there will usually be a direct, big-screen projection of the speaker. This affords the audience a much-magnified, well-lit view of every program person. The fact that these very expensive, very efficient systems exist proves the point. Audiences better attend the oral part of a communiqué when the visual part is in place.

A final word: avoid the single-spotlight-in-the-darkness kind of lighting wherever you can. From the audience's standpoint, it does enhance the drama of the communiqué. Still, for the speaker, it does little for audience feedback. Good lighting allows the audience to continue to instruct and direct the sermon. You must be able to see their faces and read their body language if you are going to make your communication a dialogue as you speak. There should be at least enough light on the audience that their reactions to the speech are discernible.

When all possibility for feedback is lost, the sermon as a living document has ceased to be. I remember a certain Midwestern university where I have lectured several times. Each time I go there I pray that God will have allowed them to better electrify their dingy lecture hall. Never in my repeated visits has God answered my prayers. So, each time I lecture there, I peer into the gray-lit hall and lecture as the poor students peer back. The house has no light, only a thousand large-pupilled eyes. Slit-eyed, we stare at each other like "squinty-faced seal-pups." If we could really see each other, squinting by the hundreds, I'm sure that we would find the whole affair most amusing. While I have lectured on that campus several times, I always leave with the feeling that I've never really ever seen anybody.

Microphones, Lecterns, and the *Sermo Corporis*

Long ago, broadcast journalists introduced us to the idea of "talking heads" on the 5:30 news. But back before that, people often used their hands when they spoke; they gestured. They moved around a bit as well. Socrates used to call this movement during communication, the *sermo corporis*, the speech of the body. Today the idea is out of vogue. Presidents and other speakers have finally learned not to gesture when making speeches. There is a possibility that much of the energy of speaking has been lost. This "talking heads" age into which we have entered has also served to make preachers and other types who do use their hands look foolishly wild.

But the total cause has not been lost. If you watch today's most popular comedians, you still see a great deal of this kind of animated speaking. This leads me to believe that those who have to make their living by communicating, and above all by storytelling, are still using a great deal of *sermo corporis*. Probably the idea still works.

Obviously, the more we use gestures and movement, the more physical space we are going to need to communicate. When this physical space is at an optimum, three issues must work together: the (standing) microphone, the lectern, and the floor-space around the two. Often the space factor can be improved on the spot. It may require something as simple as moving a couple of folding chairs or replacing the microphone. But be sure to examine this need for all minor adjustments before it is your turn to speak. Awkwardness results from trying to create this physical space as you speak.

The Real Distance and the Psychological Distance

This third step in breaking the communication barrier is one of quick but perceptive analysis. Electronic equipment can deceive us into believing that simply because the audience can hear us they will respond to us in a relational way. Not so. Relationships improve as subjects move closer to us. A few short decades ago, church architects made this discovery. It was in the 1940s and 1950s that evangelicals seemed to come alive with what architects taught them about worship. In round churches, listeners could be "en-pewed" at closer distances to the pulpit. Virtually all large churches which have constructed new buildings in the last couple of decades have gone to this style of architecture. As people have moved closer to the pulpit, their attention has intensified.

In discussing the four distances that involve us sociologically with our world, the distances are assessed in this way: twenty-five to twelve feet is the *public distance*, twelve to four feet is the *social distance*, four feet to eighteen inches is the *personal distance*, and eighteen inches to contact is the *intimate distance*. Salespersons know that everything from a used car to a tiny diamond sell within the last four feet of personal interchange. You never hear real-estate salespersons or jewelers shouting propositions or making offers across the parking lot. Good salesmanship moves closer in.

Need I go further? Communication is the language of marketing. Whatever worldview or philosophy we

THE FOUR DISTANCES

1 the public distance

2 the social distance

3 the personal distance

4 the intimate distance

are trying to promote, we must make that offer within a few short feet of relationship. But how can we? Isn't the first row of the audience often more than twenty feet from the platform? And what about all of those other rows? How can we transcend this distance?

Key Six communicators have an ability to shorten the psychological distance by transcending the actual distance: "The effectiveness is increased when it is clearly a word spoken from person to person."[51] When communication reaches a gripping efficiency, the actual distance disappears, and a psychological closeness occurs. The usual indispensable elements of power communication make it happen. Strong content, good statistics, well-told stories, and listener involvement are key.

There is one other elusive aspect of achieving the proper relational distance. I don't know what to call this aspect except "reaching." Reaching is the gap-closer in bridging all psychological distances. Reaching is a longing to communicate and be heard. It is the speaker's unconscious leaning in the direction of the audience. It is a hunger to be having a one-on-one conversation with each of them rather than having to talk to all of them at once. It is that grip in the gut that makes you break out in a cold sweat. It is your fear that they will quit listening to you before you are able to become friends with them. This *angst* wants to please an audience and give them all the usable information they need to transform their lives. It's that final longing to cross the personal thresholds that separate speaker and audience and to merge with them in communicative oneness.

What has all of this got to do with technology and electronic amplification? Just this: either the microphone system will help you achieve this intimacy or it will destroy it. Isn't this why we supposedly have microphones—to bring speaker and listener into easy conversation? A malfunctioning system shuts down this closeness. Bad mikes call attention to the fact that you are on a stage. Screaming feedback points out that you are holding a microphone, the mace of power in this potential relationship. A quality sound system promotes this relationship. When the microphone works well, it effectively disappears. Then you can enter into oneness with each separate listener.

But the slightest bit of feedback will put you right back on the stage and slams them down hard in the thirty-second row. Bad electronics doesn't just mess up a speech. It reminds the audience, suddenly and brutally, that the two of you live in different worlds. It says that you are not like them at all. It causes them to notice how you're dressed, and it reminds them that you are getting paid to say everything you are saying. Therefore, malfunctioning mikes enlarge the psychological distance between speaker and listener. They wreck identity. Then you really do become like a remote used-car salesman. You only shout your bargains across a wide lot, making all your sales quite unlikely.

Dramatic Devices and Electronic Devices

Amplifiers have for their greatest blessing their greatest fault. They amplify every sound they pick up regardless of the level at which they receive it. A whisper if amplified is a very loud whisper, thus making it accessible to the listeners. But a scream is a very loud scream. An explosive "p" or "t" sound sometimes resounds like rifle fire. Sibilants hang in the air like hissing snakes; these electronic "esses" coil unpleasantly about the ear. Speaking too closely into a microphone puts unnecessary hisses in vowel sounds. Sometimes the dynamics of a sermon will call for a "stage whisper." Do it, but beware of moving so close to the mike that the effect is a shout. And shouting? Well, remember, blessed are the merciful.

The worst performance of *King Lear* I have ever seen was done by an actor whose carefully concealed mike gave us too much sound. His drama sent us all scurrying out of the theater to stock up on Tylenol for the third act. To borrow a line from MacBeth, this performance of Lear was "full of sound and fury" signifying migraines. Mercifully, in the play, Lear at last died, and things quieted down a bit.

Preachers have sometimes been characterized as "adenoidal lungbusters." So if you have been told that "sans amplification" your voice would raise the dead, give the dead a break. Perhaps then the living will stick with you till the speech is over. If you have been used to speaking to a small crowd without amplification, you may want to experiment with sound levels before you get your "big time" communiqué underway. Always remember that the ears of your receivers are made of "itsy-bitsy," jewel-like parts. These tiny watch-like components are not meant to respond to sledge-hammer oratory. So give your audience a break. It is Christlike to leave their fragile hearing mechanism intact.

Now that we have looked at the various ways to confront the electronic barriers to communication, let us turn our attention to three other issues of Key Six communication. These elements include projection, dynamics, and listener involvement. These three aspects of "making sure they hear" are much more basic than the ins and outs of communications.

Projection: The Three Issues

Key Six communicators know how to project what they are saying. Projection is the art of getting our words "out there." The word *projection*, of course, relates with the cinema. It implies that an image has been moved from the film to a more distant and improved vantage point.

Sound projection means the same thing. Take careful note: we are no longer on the subject of microphones. We are speaking of that *sui generis* kind of projection. We are considering the all-important matter of "throwing the voice" toward the audience. Projection leaves the sermon deposited amply at the very porches of the human ear.

Note this: The speaker does this, not the sound system! Even if the speaker is using microphones, his or her words must deliver the necessary volume to the microphone. Projection is not loudness. It is in issue of energy, not decibels. Microphones may make soft speech loud, but they cannot give weak words strength. Projection is the pier of power in the communiqué. Implicit in projection are three values. Let's consider them one at a time.

The Art of Talking Loud Without Seeming To

The art of talking loud without seeming to lies in our willingness to violate our own sense of meekness. For most genteel spirits, talking loud seems not to be very couth. Loudmouths are intrusive and those who talk louder than necessary are offensive. To develop the art of projection, we must cross this bias. We must talk louder than we like to hear ourselves. One communications expert wisely counsels:

The loudness of your voice says a lot about you. We tend to think of people with meek or soft voices as being shy and timid, perhaps afraid to speak up because they're so unsure of themselves. On the other hand, people with loud, booming voices may be thought of as overbearing, overconfident, and boorish. When a person speaks too loudly, we often pull back—both physically and mentally.

To many people, the person who doesn't talk loudly enough to be easily heard is the more annoying. It's frustrating to have to continually ask a person to speak up or, even worse, to miss much of what that person says.[52]

A volume shift may seem artificial the first time or two that we do it. Before long, however, we will do a "volume shift" as soon as we utter the first words of any public speech. This volume shift must be done naturally. But beware! There is a tendency to allow other kinds of baggage to accompany the volume shift. Sometimes preachers add to the extra volume a little resonance. This "mellow reverb" intonation gives the speech a "gawdly" tone. To their way of thinking this holy, hollow, haunting, loudness has in it a touch of pseudo-Elijah. Ralph Lewis counsels us thus: "Beware a holy tone, stained-glass speech, spraying the congregation with perfumed water, or unloading the sermon in the stale fervor of a falsetto whine in an attempt to lengthen a limited personality."[53]

So be very sure that when you shift to projection, you do not add any *basso sinaitic* to your performance. It is easy to tell if you've shifted into a preacher's tone. Just listen to how long it takes you to say God. If you find yourself stretching it into two syllables, it is time to get the phony out of your phonetics.

THE 3 POSSIBLE SIDE EFFECTS OF THE VOLUME SHIFT

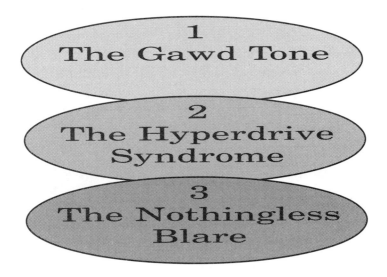

1
The Gawd Tone

2
The Hyperdrive Syndrome

3
The Nothingless Blare

The only other real baggage that can get tied on to the volume shift is the "hyperdrive syndrome." The hyperdrive syndrome is one which reasons, "If the volume shift will get them to listen, then a 'super scream' will rivet their attention." Wrong! Hearing is the reason we project. Projection is not a matter of just being loud. When I was a child, I used to sit for long periods in church. I often listened to preachers who, it seemed to me, assumed that the rest of the world was deaf. I think I know why they did it. Screaming insists that people listen, whether they want to or not. But it is better to give audiences other reasons to listen to compel their attention with uncommon loudness.

There is one final reason that preachers get loud: The nothingness blare allows the preacher to hold interest when he has nothing to say. It keeps people listening even when the content is so thin. Preachers of small preparation read the body language of their disinterested congregations. They meet this rising disinterest with homiletical horror. Volume answers vacancy. But make no mistake about it: most who listen are fully aware that the preacher's volume and content vary inversely in a sermon. So while they appear to be mesmerized by the thunder, they really crave lightning.

The Projection-Diction Ratio

Projection must be constant. If you have moments when your projection drops, your content is lost. Just as low projection kills content, so does a hurried pace. The delivery must not fly too fast. But low projection and rapid delivery can be compensated for, to some degree, by keeping a precision in your words.

Diction seems to be a lost art. In this relational day and age, when ethnic values are at an all-time high, we may be prone to preserve our particular slant on language. Therefore, we treasure dialect, even that which has a heart of poor diction. I have known Scottish preachers who picked up an entrancing dialect while on a six-week study leave at Edinburgh. Genuine dialect is a source of ethnic pride. One can hear the advertising magnates selling everything from sneakers to colas with the abundant use of dialect.

For my part, however, I would opt for speaking in what we used to call "the King's English," making our "d's" with a full and breathy break, our "f's" with our upper teeth squarely on our lower lip. We speak best exploding our "t's" with suddenness. Such phonetic form is what diction is all about. "C's" and "k's" ought to be brashly "hard." Our "x's" should be done in such a way that a good mean "k" brutally kicks an "s" out in front of it. Many newscasters take phonics and diction classes to be sure that every word they say can stand on its own. Such a lifelong study should occupy communicators as well. If we speak clearly, we shall make ourselves understood even at those moments when our volume drops nearly out of earshot. When our velocity begins to move quite fast, only good clear diction can render us understandable.

The Audience Lean

James Black reminds us: "The first essential in public speaking is that a man should make himself heard. Not to be heard is fully as bad as not to be understood. They both amount to the same thing . . . a vacuum in the pews!"[54] Again, remember that being heard and projecting are not the same thing. But when they can hear, and when they like what they are hearing, people have a tendency to lean toward us. Look for this "audience lean." Its symbol is that listeners sit on the edge of their chairs, moving as close to the speaker as they can get. It's all a psychological act of which they are almost totally unaware. It's a symbolic affliction that they can't help. But it tells you how well your projection, diction, and your content are cooperating.

Dynamics: The Two Continuums

The dynamics of any single communiqué are as multifold as there are kinds of speeches. And in so short a work, I will not attempt to define the various devices of interest that there are. But dynamics has to do with that variety of forms that steals sameness from communication. It is easier to understand the meaning of dynamics if we examine written music.

Music is written to be sung or played expressively. Musical compositions are scored in such a way that the notes, accidentals, rests, and flow of the piece are written. There are metrical symbols, sharps, flats, and time signatures that dictate how the piece will sound. But these things do not permit the piece to communicate its musical fire. The markings which cause the music to come alive are called dynamics. The dynamics are a special set of signs that tell the performer exactly what the composer had in mind when he wrote the piece. The composer intended the piece not to just be a tune, but to speak, to weep, to laugh, to frolic, to dawdle, to march, to waltz, etc. The musician cannot achieve this unless he or she reads very carefully the dynamics that tell how to make the music communicate.

Communicators have no such markings to tell them how to make their speech come alive. These dynamics must rise from the speaker's love of the subject, knowledge of the audience, and an urgent need to be heard. When all of these things are in place, then the speech, like the composition described above, will weep and laugh and sing and cry and frolic, etc. The communicator's ability to do this will be enhanced by two polarities that I like to call continuums.

The Whispering—Shouting Continuum

This set of dynamics exists to remind us that all great public speaking is conversation. I remind the pastors reading this book that the word *homily* means conversation. Conversation between any two parties is never monotone. No good friends ever hold conversation merely by exchanging information. They exchange information dynamically. They laugh; they grow solemn; they become animated. In short, they speak in everything from a whisper to a shout.

In Italy I was amazed watching Italians communicate with each other. They never did it in a monotone. They grew animated, serious, whispered, and shouted all in one five-minute greeting at a bakery. One other quality I noticed in Italy was that Italians seemed to talk as though everyone was hard of hearing and talked as though everyone around was interested.

How often while listening to a drudgerous, monotone sermon I have wished the preacher were Italian. It goes without saying that too many ministers have not learned how to employ the whisper-shouting continuum. Their communiqués suffer because they never vary the levels at which they speak. They might pick up the talent by living in the midst of people and observing how they do it. Life itself is dynamic, so if sermons have no dynamics, it may be that those who write and preach them have not touched life.

The Pause—Staccato Continuum

This continuum registers those dynamics that say that a good part of public speaking is silence. This is not a contradiction. Silence separates all spoken words. These are usually brief silences that we never really notice. But without them, no particular word would be distinguishable. It is the surrounding silence that isolates each word to allow it to hold its individual content.

But silences, in longer spaces, allow the speech to add drama and a chance for evaluation. Haddon Robinson reminds us, "The skilled speaker recognizes that pauses serve as commas, semicolons, periods, and exclamation points. Pauses are the punctuation marks of speech. Pauses are 'thoughtful silences' in speech and give the audience a brief opportunity to think, feel, and respond."[55] Speakers whose words tumble out in a hurried, inseparable fashion will weary the minds of their hearers. This is especially true if their communiqué has little content. Really insightful speeches demand pauses here and there to give their listeners a chance to "catch up."

But the most glorious use of the pause end of this continuum has to do with drama. A deliberate, worthy precept will not register in a powerful way unless there is a pause which follows the statement. Sometimes a pause on the front end of the statement will also serve. Playwrights, screenwriters, and actors certainly know this; great communicators know it as well. The great black preachers of America are masters of the one-line theme and the dramatic pause. They make use of them in their oft-repeated sermon themes. I have heard E.V. Hill of Los Angeles preach several times and each time I am amazed at the drama of his style: forceful, singular, and strong statements are always snuggling in between jabbing moments of stark, utter quiet.

Still another technique which serves well in combination with the use of pauses is staccato delivery. Staccato form in music is without any legato or slurring between notes. It is a music written in individual notes that fire at us like machine-gun bullets. This communication form, employed with pauses, rivets attention because of its crisp individualized movement.

The point of using both of these forms in one continuum is to suggest that the speed of delivery should vary just as the volume does. There will be parts of your sermon that you wish to fire at the audience in rapid syllables. This will intrigue because of its furious pace.

On the other end of this continuum, the pace may slow to a stop. The braking device for this runaway pace is the pause. But all along the pause-staccato continuum, various speeds should be used to make various points.

Listener Involvement

The Eye-Talk

There are three ways that listener feedback tells you just how interested they are in all that you are saying. The first of these is what I call "eye-talk." Hath not the poet said, "The eyes are the windows of the soul"?

D. James Kennedy of the Coral Ridge Presbyterian Church said, in reference to his personal evangelism training course: "Watch the lights to tell you how your evangelism presentation is going!" By this he means that eyes are like traffic lights. They signal any communicator on how and where to move the propositions of an argument.

A "red light," says Kennedy, is that fire in the eyes that says "Stop!" The eyes will snap this command sometimes in hostility. An "amber light" says, "Maybe I'm going to buy this communiqué and maybe I'm not. Go ahead, but proceed with caution." A "green light" on the other hand says, "Full speed ahead!"

Every communicator knows how to read the lights.

If there were no other reason for eye contact, this would be a good one. The usual idea of eye contact is that looking at people keeps them involved. But there is one other excellent reason for doing it. The eyes offer the first, best communicative feedback. Long before the rest of the body, the eyes tell you whether or not you're getting through.

The Body Silence

A second feedback evidence of listener involvement is body silence. As long as the listener's body is silent, the feedback says "I'm involved." When the body starts fidgeting and wiggling, quite another message is communicated. As we said in Key Five, this is a brutal day for speakers.

Some listeners are ruthless. Some may actually

THREE EVIDENCES OF LISTENER INVOLVEMENT

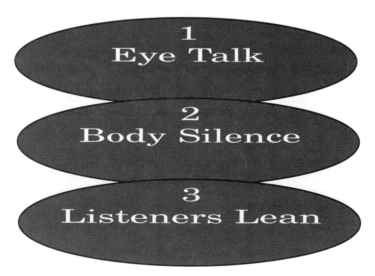

1
Eye Talk

2
Body Silence

3
Listeners Lean

stiffen their body, stand, shrug their shoulders, and walk out. This definitely is red-light communication.

In Key Five, we looked upon those whom stomp out of sermons as protesters. Here we need to see them as being more needy than belligerent. The truth is that those who make a show of leaving may be more involved in protecting themselves from the sermon than they are in arguing with it.

So on this particular kind of feedback, I offer this caveat. More and more as the culture of narcissism advances, people tend not to listen to anything which they consider offensive or not to their liking. Almost every pastor I know these days has week-to-week stories of persons who do stand up, some in obvious anger, and stomp out of the services. This may not be negative feedback, nor should these isolated occurrences be taken as a sign of poor communicative skills.

In fact, in many cases, these "gospel walk-outs" may really signal that you are communicating quite well. They may say that you've made your point "painfully" clear to them—and narcissists do not handle pain very well. They sometimes have a single anesthetic to any kind of surgery they don't like. They rise from the surgery table and stomp out of the operating room. It is often their reaction to a surgery they really need in order to get well spiritually. The surgeon should not feel badly about such obnoxious patients. They but condemn themselves.

So, contrary to the rule I am establishing here, some bodily movement (the kind that flees from your words like Ninevites before Jonah) may indicate that you are communicating very well. Ordinarily, however, such is not the case. If whole sections of the building start emptying out, this should not be taken as a sign that you have them eating out of the palm of your hand.

The Listener's Lean

One final evidence of involved listening is what we have already called the "listener's lean." Here and there when a speech is working very well you will actually see them moving toward you physically in their seats. As we have said, this listener's lean is the way their body language demonstrates ultimate interest. This joyous feedback is reflexive. It physically endorses our communiqué with the most wonderful kind of body language there is.

Reading the Feedback

Key Six communicators will read every kind of feedback that comes to them. Body language tells you not only if you are heard, but whether you are being understood. Until the spoken is audible, the reasonable remains irrational.

Everything becomes possible with projection. So I want to end this chapter with a confession and a warning. For years I had to work on a pathology of intermittent power projectors. I habitually let my voice drop into a range which, at times, is inaudible. It is a problem often diagnosed for me by older people in the audience. Sooner or later, however, it is objected to by all. I hate being told "Rev, I just couldn't hear you sometimes." But however often I have been rebuked for this sin, I always take the criticism seriously. It is, if I can look at it right, a kind of compliment. It implies that they feel that they were missing something. So, I am, in a way, grateful for the criticism.

The answer to correcting any projection problem can only be corrected as it happens. This is the hardest kind of problem to correct. While I am absorbed in the business of communicating, it is most difficult to train my ear to measure the volume of my voice. In fact, to work on the problem at all means that I must have every sermon so well prepared that I can say what I have to say as I can listen to myself say it. If I am caught in some preparedness crunch that keeps me tied to my notes, I will never be able to run my mind on that second track of listening to correct my flawed projection.

This problem seems to me to issue from two possible places. First it may come from an awesome psychological insecurity that causes us to drop our volume. We do this because in our own minds we have already dropped our level of self-esteem. We have mentally told ourselves we have little of value that anyone would be interested in hearing. Usually, these kinds of self-esteem issues do not require counseling to make us talk louder, but they do require a constant reminder that we need to do it. Thus, the second track of our mind which is not involved in communicating must constantly measure, rebuke, and order our psychological mechanism to "turn up the sound."

This kind of psychological problem may also be something left over from adolescence. It may come from the day-to-day management of the church in which uncomplimentary laypersons criticize us. Pastors rarely get a lot of good news about themselves. Carl Jung is reported to have said that it takes nine "kudos" to balance out every criticism in life. If that is the case, it is easy to believe that ministers rarely ever have a happy day. Therefore, the negative luggage they must carry into the pulpit is heavy. This burden first steals their passion and later their sermon volume. There is probably no reasonable way to hope that in this me-first age we will ever get any more positive congregational affirmation. The only answer to getting more muscle in our whipped psyches is to deepen the spiritual disciplines by which Christ himself strengthens us in the inner person.

Other projection problems haunt those who may be psychologically secure. These, however, have a naturally soft communication style. Their weak projection is rooted in soft-spokenness. This particular problem is not psychologically seated. It is not easy to deal with. It is difficult for the soft-spoken to trump up a more bombastic style. It takes a great deal of monitoring to put strength in a weak style.

Key Six communication means that we want to be heard and we will be heard. And when we are heard, we become a channel for a flow of life-changing possibilities. Until there is ample volume, communication does not get started.

For me, I learned the lesson that dark night so long ago when I stood at the front of a large crowd where the electricity was gone. All possibility of my being an "audio smash" was eliminated. I knew the question of whether to stop or go on was not the primary question. In such moments, there is only one real question. Everything depends on that question. So I stood and shouted it out over the crowd. My important, loud question rocketed into the darkness. It flew like a certain courier out over the shadowy forms before me: "Can you hear?" And from the darkness, a kind voice shouted back the only words that can make any sermon possible: "Preach on!"

And so I did.

Key Seven:

Killing Interest-Lag Through the Six Values of Mobility

Speak the speech, I pray you,

as I pronounced it to you,

trippingly on the tongue.[56]

The Audience Challenge of

Key Seven

Dear Speaker:

I always feel sorry for a preacher who is flounderin' on his feet. Everybody does. There they are, talking along through a snoring sea of nodding narcoleptics, knowing they're not cuttng the mustard. Furthermore, they know we know. It's like watching the crash and burn of an airliner in slow motion. You know where it's all going to end and you can't do a thing to stop it. Preachers have to fail so publicly.

I was at an African-American service the other day when a poor monotone European-American was boring us out of our gourds. One hefty brother, toward the back of the service, kept saying, "Help him, Jesus! Help him, Jesus!" Jesus didn't. I don't know why Jesus didn't help him. We all would have if we could.

Still I've seen it happen a lot of times. You think when they're up there preaching God's Word, He'd help 'em out of the mess that they sometimes get themselves in. Everybody would appreciate it. But God just kind of watches a poor sermon go up in smoke, shaking His head like the rest of us.

I've always wondered why, when a preacher knows he's not doing it, why he just doesn't bless everybody and send them off to the cafeterias early. A surgeon will stop her surgery when she knows her patient has died on the operating table. A boxer will leave the ring once the fight is over and the arena is empty. A cowboy will dismount when he knows for sure his horse is dead. Only preachers keep on preaching after they've run out of sermon. Darndest thing. They just won't quit. In all my years of church-going, I've never heard a soul criticize preachers for preaching short sermons, only vice-versa. Anyway, if I were you, I'd quit preaching just before we quit listening. If not, don't expect God to come down and deliver you. He won't do it. You'll be up there failing all by yourself with everybody lookin' on. If you do it very often, maybe you should get another job.

—Your Audience

Successful public speakers are not just those with the best content, physical energy, or eye contact. The best communicators are those who can adjust either their content or delivery style to meet the situation. The best speaker can seize upon any unexpected happenstance and turn it to a communicative advantage. This kind of talent implies a free-style delivery. Such rare and easy speakers can alter or scuttle content and form to preserve the general interest. This whole "hang-loose" mystique realizes that no communication can occur after people quit listening. Therefore, such communicators best prove their mettle by adjusting their communiqués in process. They are able, at a moment's notice, to resnag all interrupted audience attention.

Just as a great hitter learns to adjust his batting stance to accommodate a particular pitcher, a great communicator adjusts his pitch to accommodate a particular audience. No two games are ever alike. A tense inning requires a tense attitude. A comfortable lead can inspire overconfidence. A bases-loaded, two-out event puts a different kind of money on coming to bat. There is both the necessity of looking over the ball and measuring whether to step up to it or back away from it. In this final chapter, we will look at what must be done to win at keeping interest. Switch hitting in communication is as important to winning as it is in baseball.

Much of this book has to do with preventing interest-lag. This chapter alone, the seventh key, has to do with killing it. This final key may be the most strategic key of all. For in spite of all that we can do, we cannot always prevent interest-lag. Once it shows up, we must begin our own private war to stamp it out.

We have already discussed many evidences. It begins in audience restlessness, often with children. Yawns proliferate. Slack jaws appear often, first among the golden agers. Narcoleptic executives surface. Then there are glazed eyes and nodding heads. Drooping eyelids, nail-filing, advanced gum chewing. All these signal the communicator that he or she isn't. Mobility is lost.

We tend to watch only moving objects. Take a ping-pong ball. It is almost humorous to observe a group of people watching a table-tennis game. The methodical movement of the eyes as the eggy white ball clicks across the table, the eyes of the watchers snap to and fro, from end to end, mechanically, like wind-up mechanisms. Why? Because the ball is moving; lay that same ball on the table, and all would lose interest.

The mobility issue of communication is the key to the interest factor. Seneca has well pointed out that the difference between a pond and a stream is the issue of mobility. Streams move; ponds stagnate. Streams intrigue; ponds disinterest. We like to put our feet in streams; we are afraid of putting our feet in ponds! Great communiqués are streams; dull sermons are ponds.

But how do we act to keep our communiqués mobile? To be short about it, we must prepare very well what we are going to say. Generally speaking, preparation prevents interest-lag and promotes mobility. Poor preparation promotes a stolid style. Preachers who are known as communicators will often spend one hour in the study for every one minute they spend in the pulpit. Preparation generally concerns itself with content, but for those who really want to hold an audience, preparation must also concern itself with dynamics and delivery. Good preparation must always use some of its time to rehearse the various components of delivery. Craig Loscalzo reminds us of this when he says that "the key to effective preaching is for you to remember that preaching is a dynamic event that requires you to use effectively all your skills of communication; your voice, your gestures, your personality, your spirit, your total self."[57] As we rehearse communication forms, interest-lag dies and power communication takes place.

"Out loud" is the glory of rehearsal. Until we practice our sermon out loud we have no idea how it really sounds. And out loud is the only way our audience will ever hear it. They will never know how great our outline was, or how fine the manuscript is. They will judge all by the only facet they can know: its outloudness.

Out loud is the joy of mobility. In attending church during my teen years, I would often watch the big hand of the church's wall clock: it did not move fast, but always faster than the sermon. I always wondered what would happen if my pastor's sermon had been constructed as intricately as that clock. The clock had gears and springs and a hundred tiny, inner evidences that it had been carefully put together. His sermon seemed unmade, a hapless meandering through the vacant halls of Tuesday's mind. The clock of course had mobility. The sermon, like an inert, silent ping-pong ball, was immobile. His homily lay in dead syllables, old precepts, and thumb-worn illustrations I had heard before—back when I was more interested. He walked around some in the chancel, but his sermon never did anything. It just laid there, refusing to get up and move. It was so dead that all hope of resurrection was impossible. Gratefully, in the summer, the windows were open and flies buzzed by. Anything that moved in our church was welcome.

Mobility is a stream. It is communication that flies so fast that it defies interest-lag. The key, of course, is to start the sermon moving and keep it moving. But for even the best communicators, the pace sometimes slows down, in spite of all we can do. The room may be too warm. Dawdling hymns may have so hypnotized the audience that they never quite recovered from the four-minute offertory prayer. God Himself seems asleep. The stream of communication mobility puddles up in a sleepy pool of boredom. But what are we to do when interest-lag sets in? When we see all these things die as we sermonize, we must do something to kill it even as we preach. We must get things moving once again. But how? How are we to bring life to deadness? Let me offer these six stimuli to restoring mobility to a crawling, stumbling sermon.

The Great Gamble: Changing Everything on the Spot

Throwing out a malfunctioning sermon on the spot will create immediate interest! This stimulus usually dramatically improves the immobility. The problem with the technique is that the express lane that we have chosen is usually under construction. Therefore, it is not in a ready state of travel. This means that while things may move fast for a while they may not go very far.

So the hazards are immense. It is not merely interest-lag that motivates this response. Sometimes, we can be overwhelmed by the feeling that we have chosen the right sermon for the wrong crowd. One of the advantages of long-term pulpit experience is that it affords us a file of back-up materials if we need to change our sermon on the spot.

For the last decade, I have carried the same Bible into every pulpit with me. Throughout half-a-thousand speaking engagements I have not changed Bibles. This Bible contains twenty outlines of oft-used sermons that permit me a way out of the morass of a non-mobile preaching event. Some years ago, I was preaching a series of Sunday evening sermons on the incarnation. On a particular Sunday afternoon, word came to me that the chairman of trustees for our congregation had been tragically killed in an auto accident. This church servant was so popular that the whole church was grieved by his death. I knew that to preach on something as remote as I had planned wouldn't fly. In the face of such extreme group pain, I wanted to be relevant. That night I turned from the text at hand and preached from one of the twenty other outlines that had been in my Bible for a long time. This new sermon was one I often used at funerals. It dealt with God's exaltation of the obedient life, and it worked well.

But I must confess that here and there I have changed on the spot from a sermon I knew was boring to one that I hoped would not be. I had to gamble that the new and less prepared sermons would do at least as well as the one I was abandoning to regain interest.

This entire sermon switch-out is more important for pastors who have been leading the same congregation for years. The newness of visiting speakers allows them to get by with weak content easier than a long-term pastor might. Long-term pastors must have compelling content. This also makes the sermon switch very critical. We must be careful. Trying to replace a "fizzler" with a "sizzler" has its hazards. What we switch to must not have been used either too recently or frequently before.

Sermon switching is an issue of radical surgery. It should be used only if it is clear that the patient will die without it. Such a radical suggestion makes it clear that my whole philosophy of communication sets as priority, the issue of audience interest. The stakes of the great gamble are immense! But any risk is better than boredom. The big switch could also mire down in immobility. But even if it does, it will be no worse than the original communiqué. So proceed cautiously. Wisdom must be justified of her children. Let us, however, move on to other, less drastic stimuli for killing interest-lag.

The Lesser Gamble: Changing What Isn't Working on the Spot

The second antidote to interest-lag is less radical. The desperate surgery of a massive "sermonectomy" may not be necessary. Sometimes the removal of an infected illustration will allow the sick sermon to get well. The simple laserectomy of an old poem may prevent the need for major surgery. Still, changing your sermon in any way, during delivery, requires care. You can snip too much and overcut. You may not have enough clamps for the massive sutures. The sermon could die on the operating table.

I once was the pastor of a poor man who went into the hospital to have his tonsils out. When he came out from under the anesthetic he found his nose plastered with bandages. He had to be told by his careless surgeon that they had misread his chart. They had made a mistake and taken his adenoids out. What's to be done? Trying to amend a sick sermon can cause us to cut too recklessly. Bits of homiletic this-and-that lying about the operating room will signal our failure. When such surgery is over, we may lament our over-hasty snipping. But all of us can sense when we are laboring to cauterize a part of the sermon we probably should amputate.

Amending the sermon in progress depends upon our being sensitive. We must be able to spot what has gone wrong or what is going wrong. The worst part is that this analysis must be done even as we speak. I have seen speakers lost in the rapture of quoting a poem whose rapture somehow eluded their listeners. I remember a young singer who was attempting to quote the doggerel lines of "The Old Violin." His quote sheets became so mixed, that "The Old Violin," which always takes a long time to quote, went on for eternity. The poor man's sheets were so scrambled that we passed the auction scene in the poem several times while he frantically sorted through his notes. When he asked for the fifth time, "What am I bid for the old violin?" I was tempted to bid out loud. I felt elated! If my bid was adequate to buy the old violin, I could destroy it and protect all future generations from hackneyed homiletics.

I remember another preacher who spent forty-five minutes telling the none-too-fascinating tale of his wife's search for her natural birthmother. Imagine our disappointment in listening to the tale for all that time, and finding out that the poor woman never found her lost mother. It was a very unhappy ending which perfectly fit a very unhappy story. What amazed me in both of these cases was that the speak-

er droned on and on without the slightest understanding that they were boring their audience into
the ground.

In my early years as a preacher, I developed a
three-star sermon on Naaman, the leper. It would
have been a four-star sermon except for the plodding
pace that the sermon kept. In the sermon, I likened
leprosy to sin. This is not all that unusual when anyone speaks of leprosy, but as a part of the sermon I
had also developed a lengthy description of the dis-
ease. This sermonic diagnosis discussed how the dis-
ease is transmitted along with its early detection and
treatment. Sometimes I had the feeling that I was
really communicating and the audiences were spell-
bound. At other times I felt that I was telling them
more about leprosy than they really wanted to know.
During my latter pulpit years, I have shortened the
leprosy sermon to keep its boring contagion from
spreading.

It is important to make each sermon a living document whose preached insights keep closely in touch
with the audience's interest. When it lags, sermon
therapy or surgery must quickly begin.

Pulling from Your
Accessible Back File

The proper use of illustrations is a key to power
communication. As W. E. Sangster so aptly put it: "At
any level of persuasion, illustration is the preacher's
help. A vivid picture that clarifies thought, or a feel-
ingful story that touches the emotion, both (in their
different ways) thrust at the resisting will . . . what-

ever branch of preaching it be, skill in the use of illustration means more power in the effort to persuade."[58] But are we sensitive enough to know when our sermon illustrations are not communicating?

Finding the weak spots is not as hard as strengthening them, of course. Strengthening them means that as you cut, you must also transplant a new sermon prosthesis. As in all surgery, it is easier to remove the problem than to find a functional replacement. There are three donors which make such transplants possible: the trick, the napalm file, and the old illustration back list. Let's examine them one at a time.

Using Old Files

This is a prosthesis that often doesn't fit the amputated organ. In fact, it is so ill-fitting that most of the audience will be keenly aware you have switched. Do they mind? It all depends on how boring the item is which you are abandoning. A bad fit usually bothers the speaker more than the speakee. Most people would rather sit through an interesting disjuncture than boring symmetry. For the next few paragraphs, I want to refer to this trade-off as the trick.

The trick has for its greatest asset the fact that it is a part of your memorized back-list. It is therefore easily accessible to your memory. It's there when you need it. It's like a surgeon who, going in to do an appendectomy, notices that he really needs to do a kidney transplant. If the patient is going to live, he must face a radical change of procedures. Happily he sees that he has a kidney "in the can." To be sure, it is overlarge and a bit ill-fitting. Still, he finds he can sew it in and save the patient.

But all such sermon surgery does not always have a happy outcome. Sometimes a loss of equilibrium cannot be corrected. There are not enough tricks to replace every infected organ. So there is nothing left to do but to lose some patients on the operating table. Following this humble sense of hacking our homiletics to ruin, we vow to start earlier on the next week's sermon. One thing is for sure; there are not enough tricks to paste together to compensate for consistently poor preparation.

Using the Napalm File

The napalm file is much less accessible than the trick. To use this file at all will demand that you must be able to sense ahead of time those places where your sermon is weak. The napalm file is a gathering of sermon illustrations so hot that they can be used almost anywhere. The weakness of napalm material is that it usually doesn't fit very well. Those who listen to the sermon will probably find themselves fascinated. But they may wonder what in the world the hot illustration had to do with the sermon. The material is only justifiable if we recall that interest is always preferred above boredom.

I have repeatedly justified anything which holds interest, and perhaps before I move on, I had best make it clear that the most preferable kind of communication is that which both interests and contributes to the sermon's unity. Long-range preparation is all that will ensure this thoughtful approach. Nothing is to be more celebrated than a sermon which has unity and symmetry—where all information coheres and contributes. The goal is to make every illustration a

THREE WAYS TO ACCESS
A BACKFILE

1 ⇨ THE TRICK

2 ⇨ THE NAPALM FILE

3 ⇨ THE STANDBY ILLUSTRATION FILE

napalm illustration which is both "hot" and also "fits." And the best way to build such intense, well-crafted sermons is to craft carefully ahead of time.

Using the Standby Illustration File

This brief file, like the napalm file, is a list of catalogued illustrations. It is merely a list of illustration titles. But the illustrations are quite familiar. Only the titles are needed to suggest entire illustrations that you have used effectively before. You know that these illustrate well. You know they will communicate.

I have about two hundred of these titled illustrations that appear in an alphabetized and catalogue listing. They are not all stories. There are memorized quotes, quips, poems, and poem fragments. When I'm doing any series as a guest preacher or lecturer, I keep this list close at hand. Like my American Express card, I never leave home without it.

Because much of my public speaking is done in the form of sermons, I have entered much of this standby illustration file in the front and back pages of my Bible. By having it actually in my Bible I am able to refer to it even as I preach. I feel safe having it at hand. I turn to it when I feel my sermon getting caught in the ugly clutches of audience disinterest.

Casually (Not Desperately) Asking for Attention

Always asking for attention means that we will get that attention in diminishing returns. The number of times that we ask for it, and the number of times that we get it, will vary inversely. I have a Methodist friend who, after reading this chapter, may not be a friend. Still, he is always saying, "Listen up, folks!" The phrase is so annoyingly frequent that it is almost a vocalized pause! By definition, a vocalized pause is "a meaningless word or grunt." We use these as fillers in those silent places where we really have nothing to say. Years ago when the phrase began to inhabit his sermon, people probably did "listen up." But now they no longer hear his command to listen. All too often they no longer hear his sermon. I know a preacher in a sister denomination who punctuates lagging interest by saying, "Hear me. This is very important!" The problem with the phrase is that it implies that the undesignated parts of his sermons aren't so important.

Does a mid-sermon demand to "listen up" ever work? Perhaps it is when used once or twice in a sermon or when it really is followed by very strong material. If we ask them to listen, just so we can have their attention, we have asked them to serve our self-interest. If, however, we ask them to listen because we are going to give them relevant, usable information, then we have made the sermon their servant. We have not only been honest in asking for their attention, we have been truly pastoral.

One of the most moving sermons I have ever heard was from a homeless person. He wandered into our small church on a Sunday morning when I was a pastor in Plattsmouth, Nebraska. He startled me by walking to the pulpit and asking everyone to listen to his story. I was reluctant to do so for I feared his impromptu sermon would leave no place for my own. But after he began, I became convinced that his was better than mine. His plea for the audience to listen was well given. Our attention was also well given.

But for the most part we should never ask for attention. Such asking is not only a sign we don't have it, it is also probably an evidence we don't deserve it. The request will only remind our audience that we have failed them in a very significant way.

Heightening Projection

Getting louder does get attention. We spoke of the dangers of this technique in chapter 6. This device will only work so long as we don't have to get loud and stay loud because the sermon is weak all the way through. Volume, however, is a valid tool of power communication. It is a component of good technique but should not be all that the sermon is based on. Al Fasol wisely reminds us, "The excessive volume patterns among preachers have been caused by the fallacy that preaching is suspect unless it is loud. The cure is to realize that volume is a servant of content. The speaker should therefore use force or abstain from it as content dictates."[59] We should use volume wisely and appropriately, since it is an important means of communication until its abuse becomes ear-splitting.

There are some exceptions to the normal rule when the circumstances themselves become abnormal. For instance, I recently found myself lecturing in a large college fieldhouse on a Southern campus. Right after I began speaking, a terrible rainstorm occurred. The sound of the rain on the roof was suddenly a roar. Rather than be drowned out, no pun intended, I raised my volume and kept going for the better part of a half-hour. I'm still not sure it was smart to continue speaking during the deluge. Sometimes it is obviously better to stop and dismiss. But at least for those who wanted to pay attention, attention was possible because of my heightened projection.

Occasionally I have heard a speaker initiate dialogue between two characters, where the effect of using one loud voice and one quiet voice captivates the audience because of the contrast. Such loud projection kills interest-lag, which is generally not done for that reason. Reading a biblical character such as that of a prophet can also achieve this. Telling the story of Nathan's rebuke of David would work very well dramatically if the prophet's rebuke was almost shouted, "Thou art the man" (2 Sam. 12:7). Sensibility must dictate the matter. Overdone, it could be melodrama.

Quitting Early

When preaching, it is important to remember to take only as much time as needed to make our point. Thinning the content by lengthening our communiqué may stretch our message beyond its elasticity. In his preaching book, *Between Two Worlds*, John R. W. Stott counsels us: "I think every sermon should last just as long as the preacher needs in which to deliver his soul. Basically, it is not the length of a sermon which makes the congregation impatient for it to stop, but the tedium of a sermon in which even the preacher himself appears to be taking very little interest."[60]

With Dr. Stott's comment as a backdrop, let me state that the final way to restore interest-lag is to simply admit that I've nothing more to say. It is generally best to admit this only to one's psyche and not to the audience in general. I personally find that people rarely get angry because preachers quit early. Needless to say, it is better to quit nearer the end of the sermon than its beginning. But if interest-lag is too terminal to correct, a quick wrap-up may seem heaven-sent. Be as clever with the exit as you can be. Pray that the choir has a dazzling seven-fold amen after the benediction. Two specific circumstances come quickly to mind.

The first was when a furious week of ministry had stung my sermon preparation time into paralysis. This occurred back when I was still young. I had no "brown-and-serve" file. I was barely five minutes into my sermon when I realized I had rushed headlong into a hopeless filibuster with no significant content. I tried to preach for four or five more minutes with nothing of glory coming across my mental teleprompter. I too thought of quoting "The Old

Violin," but I had already done it twice during other recent dying homilies.

As I struggled to keep the sinking sermon afloat, I prayed for the apocalypse. It was not forthcoming. I thought of launching into the 119th Psalm, and trying to convince them it was my very favorite seven-page psalm. I thought about giving the long version of my testimony, but I had done that during another stalled sermon only a few months earlier. A baby cried. A fly buzzed by. A chirping cricket was getting more attention than I was. Finally, I had to just be honest and conclude like Porky Pig, "That's all, folks."

One old layman rebuked me for not earning my money. By and large, however, most of them seemed grateful that they would beat the Methodists to the cafeteria. I went home from church determining that I would keep them longer the next Sunday. It was the only time I quit right after the introduction to my sermon. At least two or three times per year, however, I have admitted to myself that I was through and so blessed them with an early benediction.

The second instance that comes to mind occurred shortly after I joined the faculty at the seminary. As I was lecturing in a certain class, no hands were going up and no questions were coming in; in short, there was nothing to impede the break-neck speed with which I was gobbling up the pages of my lecture. After twenty minutes, I was through. Once again, I had that nauseating feeling that my audience had beat me to the finish line. I wrapped up the brief lecture amid wild cheering. They left class joyously. But I dragged out and shuffled morosely back to my office. I determined to write a longer lecture for the next day. On this very sad walk along the *via dolorosa* hallway, I met a colleague. He too was shuffling along, doing nothing much except mumbling his own *mea culpas*.

"What's the matter, Dr. B?" I asked. "Oh," he replied, "I ran out of lecture early." Misery loves company. I felt great. I was comforted in knowing that his sins were mine, for he had been teaching for years.

I'm convinced that the best time to quit talking is at that exact moment you run out of something to say. Sermons in some ways are like people. Some die in old age. Some die in infancy. But blessed is either the person or the sermon which dies while someone still loves and misses it.

A Call to Passion

It has been forty years since I was a teenager working on my sister's farm in Pond Creek, Oklahoma. But the night the First Christian Church burned in Pond Creek, I remember that I joined the rest of the small Oklahoma hamlet to watch the blaze. We watched, fixed with a sense of sadness and yet utter fascination. It was not possible to go home. It was traitorous to leave the work of saving the church to the fire department. We all stayed and watched till the church was consumed. Orange flames held our vision. Fire crackled as the great supporting timbers crashed downward.

I am sure that so many who stood watching the church burn were delinquent members. The church hadn't held much intrigue for them until it caught fire. Interest-lag always suffers from a lack of fire. John Wesley reportedly said, "Let a man get on fire for God, and people will come to watch him burn."

When churches burn they attract a large crowd. When pastors are aflame with vision, they also attract a crowd. A lack of fire, however, always creates several feet-of-pew-per-worshiper. Bad sermons provide utter spaciousness. But they have a worse fault. They keep listeners separated from their well-deserved unity with God. Poor communication finds commentary in the little lady who said to her pastor: "Preacher, your sermons are so bad that they deprive me of peace and quiet while they furnish me no companionship."

Years ago I decided the call to preach was a call to passionate living. Really it was more than that: it was a call to passionate being. All of my sermons do not catch fire. Many lamentably smoulder waiting for the Spirit who hides Himself. But here and there those who get proficient at using the seven keys of communication will grow so adept at unlocking audiences that they will call down an Acts 2 kind of fire.

Such sermonic fire still gathers a wonderful crowd. How blessed are those incendiary communicators whose verbal arson sets their world aflame with interest.

Chapter Outlines

Key One

Relationship Is Everything
>First Impressions
>The First Three Minutes
>The Speech-Before-the-Speech
>The Critical Warm-up

Three Issues of Relationship
>Here's How I'm Like You!
>Here's Why We Need Each Other!
>Here's Why I'm Here! Here's Why You're Here!

Audience Analysis

The Speaker's Credentials
>What I've Learned
>How Long I Took to Learn It
>Ways I've Found It to Be True
>How You Can Learn It Faster

Making Friends

Key Two

Receiving Power from Your Audience
> Speaking on Their Behalf
> Burying Your Lead

Four Evidences You Have Broken the Ego Barrier
> Demonstrating Apparent Ease
> Demonstrating Humility
> Demonstrating Transparency
> Demonstrating the Ability to Laugh at Yourself

The Grand Evidences That You Are Speaking on Their Behalf
> Avoiding the Rhetoric of Selfish Power
> Working Developmentally to Keep Their Interest

Being Sensitive

Key Three

Why Should We Listen?
> Is It Important?
> Is It Entertaining?
> Is It Classic?

Stating the Promise

Making the Promise the Single Point of the
Sermon

Making the Promise Short

Making It Reasonable

Reasonable Means Logical

Reasonable Means Applicable

Reasonable Means Within Reach

Reasonable Means Something They Can
Appropriate Now

The Four Forms of Content

The Precept—The Path of Reason

The Statistics—The Path of Proof

Story—The Path of Intrigue

The Inductive Lead

The Wrap

Key Four

Story Narration

Augustine's *Narratio*

Suspense Before Revelation

Resolution: *Finis Benedictus*

Happy Ending—Tolkien's Challenge

The Post-Sermonic Mood

The Resolution Triptych

Key Five

Developing the Pyramid
> Preparation
>
> Oratorical Improvement
>
> Venture
>
> Audience Sensitivity

Truth
> Truth as Fact
>
> Truth as Experience
>
> Truth as Transference

Interest
> Let Me Entertain You
>
> Let Me Instruct You
>
> Let Me Help You to Apply This Truth

Inspiration
> Why Should Your Moods Borrow from Mine?
>
> Why Should You Be Intensely Involved?
>
> Why Is Decision Your Only Choice?

Key Six

The Use of Technology in Communication
> Lighting and Hearing: The Psychological
> Ears of the Eyes

Key Seven

Endnotes

Chapter 1

1. William Shakespeare, *A Midsummer Night's Dream*, II, ii, 27–30.

2. William Shakespeare, *Julius Caesar,* III, ii, 100.

3. J. Michael Sproule, *Communication Today* (Glenview, Ill.: Scott, Foresman, 1949), 105.

4. Ibid., 95.

5. Reg Grant and John Reed, *The Power Sermon* (Grand Rapids: Baker, 1993), 154.

6. John L. Vohs and G. P. Mohrman, *Audiences, Messages, Speakers* (New York: Harcourt Brace and Jovanovich, 1975), 48–60.

7. Lewis Carroll, *The Best of Lewis Carroll, Through the Looking Glass* (Secaucus, N.J.: Castle, a division of Book Sales, Inc., 1983), 277.

Chapter 2

8. William Shakespeare, *Hamlet,* III, ii, 69–71.

9. Martin Cooper, *Analyzing Public Discourse* (Prospect Heights, Ill.: Waveland Press, 1989), 81.

10. Nan Kilkeary, *The Good Communicator* (Evanston, Ill.: Quikread, 1987), 10.

11. Arnt Halvorson, *Authentic Preaching* (Minneapolis: Augsbury Publishing House, 1982), 19.

12. David Evans, *Executive Speeches* (Mass.: Brent Filson Williamstone Publishing, 1991), 26.

13. Ibid., 27.

14. Ibid., 57.

15. Daniel O' Keefe, *Persuasion: Theory and Research* (Newbury Park, Calif.: Size Publications, 1990), 140.

16. W. F. Strong, *Persuasion: Strategies for Speakers* (Dubuque, Iowa: Kendall/Hunt Publishing, 1990), 30.

17. John Oman, as cited in *Persuasive Preaching Today* (Ann Arbor, Mich.: Ralph Lewis Letho Crafters, Inc., 1979), 13.

18. Edward Markquart, *The Quest for Better Preaching* (Minneapolis: Augsbury Publishing House, 1988), 58.

19. Harold Freeman, *Varieties of Biblical Preaching* (Dallas, Tex.: Word, 1987), 173.

20. Haddon W. Robinson, *Biblical Preaching* (Grand Rapids, Mich.: Baker Book House, 1980), 187.

21. Brent Filson, *Executive Speeches* (Williamstone, Mass.: Williamstone Publishing 1991), 51.

22. John MacArthur, Jr., et. al. *Rediscovering Expository Preaching* (Dallas, Tex.: Word, 1992), 321.

23. Kathleen Kelly Reardon, *Persuasion, Theory and Context* (Beverly Hills, Calif.: Sage Publishing, 1981), 145.

24. Calvin Miller, *Spirit, Word, and Story* (Dallas, Tex.: Word, 1989), 209.

Chapter 3

25. William Shakespeare, *Pericles,* II, ii, 85–86.

26. Ralph Lewis, *Persuasive Preaching Today,* 2nd rev. ed. (Ann Arbor, Mich.: Lithocrafters, Inc. 1979), 194.

27. Thomas G. Long, *The Witness of Preaching* (Louisville, Ky.: Westminster/John Knox, 1989), 15.

28. George Barna, *The Power of Vision* (Ventura, Calif.: Regal Books, 1992), 52.

29. Fred B. Craddock, *As One Without Authority* (Nashville, Tenn.: Abingdon Press, 1979), 105.

30. Al Fasol, *Essentials of Biblical Preaching* (Grand Rapids, Mich.: Baker Book House, 1989, 52.

31. John A. Broadus, *On the Preparation of Delivery of Sermons,* revised by Jesse B. Heatherspoon (New York: Harper & Row, 1944), 94.

32. Thomas G. Long, *The Witness of Preaching* (Louisville, Ky.: Westminster/John Knox Press, 1989), 147.

33. Daniel J. O'Keefe, op. cit., 168.

34. Calvin Miller, op. cit., 139–95.

35. Ralph Lewis and Gregg Lewis, *Inductive Preaching* (Westchester, Ill.: Crossway Books, 1983), 35.

Chapter 4

36. William Shakespeare, *Richard II*, V, ii, 1–2.

37. F. Scott Fitzgerald, from "NoteBooks," in Edmund Wilson, ed., *The Crackup* (1945); quoted in John Bartlett, *Familiar Quotations,* 14th ed., edited by Emily Morrison Beck (Boston: Little, Brown, 1968), 1037. Quoted in Reg Grant and John Reed, *The Power Sermon* (Grand Rapids, Mich: Baker Books, 1993), 121.

38. Grant and Reed, op. cit., 121.

39. Rudolph F. Verderber, *Communicate!* (Belmont, Calif.: Wadsworth Publishing Company, 1981), 231.

40. Sidney Greidanus, *The Modern Preacher and the Ancient Text* (Grand Rapids, Mich.: William B. Eerdmans Publishing Company, 1988), 148.

41. Donald Coggan, *Preaching: The Sacrament of the Word* (New York: The Crossroad Publishing Company, 1987), 114.

42. John P. Newport, *Life's Ultimate Questions* (Dallas, Tex.: Word Publishing, 1989), 329.

Chapter 5

43. William Shakespeare, *The Rape of Lucrece,* lines 939–43.

44. Fred B. Craddock, *Preaching* (Nashville, Tenn.: Abingdon Press, 1985), 71.

45. David Buttrick, *Homiletic, Moves and Structures* (Philadelphia: Fortress Press, 1987), 454.

46. W. F. Strong and John A. Cook, *Persuasion Strategies for Speakers,* 2nd ed. (Dubuque, Iowa: Kendall/Hung

Publishers, 1990), 50.

47. James D. Berkley, *Preaching to Convince*, ed. Leadership Library Volume B, (Dallas, Tex.: Word Books, 1986), 70.

48. Craig A. Loscalzo, *Preaching That Connects* (Downers Grove, Ill.: InterVarsity Press, 1992), 113–14.

49. Berkley, op. cit., 29.

Chapter 6

50. William Shakespeare, *Much Ado About Nothing,* II, iii, 17–21.

51. *Preaching for Growth* (St. Louis: CBP Press, 1988), 36.

52. Jeffrey C. Hahner, et.al. *Speaking Clearly: Improving Voice and Diction* (New York: Random House, 1984), 45.

53. Ralph Lewis, op. cit., 69.

54. James Black, *The Mystery of Preaching* (Grand Rapids, Mich.: Zondervan Publishing, rev. 1977), 105.

55. Haddon W. Robinson, op. cit., 206.

Chapter 7

56. William Shakespeare, *Hamlet*, III, ii, 1–2.

57. Craig A. Loscalzo, op. cit., 153.

58. William E. Sangster, *The Craft of Sermon Illustration* (Grand Rapids, Mich.: Baker Books, 1973), 21.

59. Al Fasol, *A Guide to Self Improvement in Sermon Delivery* (Grand Rapids, Mich.: Baker Books, 1983), 63.

60. John R.W. Stott, *Between Two Worlds* (Grand Rapids, Mich.: William B. Eerdmens, 1982), 292.

Glossary

Audience lean. The listener's attempt to move as close as possible to an interesting speaker. (p. 177)

Audience power. Power the audience confers on a speaker after trust has been established and after listeners sense that the communicator is speaking on their behalf. (p. 6, 45)

Augustine's *narratio*. Technique of compelling hearers to listen by attracting them with a story. (p. 116)

Buried lead. The speaker's indirect approach to the main issue of the communiqué. (p. 47)

Communication. An interchange of thought from the mind of a sender to that of a receiver. (p. 13)

Conferred power. Power the speaker received from God or from the audience. (p. 4)

Dynamis. Power from God for any purpose that God may wish to use to accomplish His ends in His world. (p. 6)

Ego barrier. Communication block that separates the speaker from the audience when the speaker tries to impose his agenda on listeners. The empowered communicator steps across this ego barrier to speak on behalf of the audience. (p. 44)

Inductive lead. Approach to the audience in which the speaker couches the Key Three promise as a question, giving listeners premises and letting them decide for themselves. (p. 100)

Key Three promise. The speaker's promise to listeners made early in the communiqué that, if they listen, the communicator will expound to them usable information. (p. 85)

Key. Any of the seven bases of communication. (p. 1)

Lowry loop. The tension-and-release mechanism whereby the inductive process of narrative supplies the techniques of tension through gentle induction. (p. 109)

Napalm files. A collection of highly usable sermon illustrations. (p. 198)

Narratio. See **Augustine's *narratio.***

Power. See *Dynamis*.

Projection-diction ratio. Relation between a speaker's ability to project the speech and the rapidity of delivery. (p. 176)

Projection. The speaker's art of getting words "out there" so that the audience can hear them clearly. (p. 173)

Pyramid of priorities. Pyramid formed of the three priorities of Key Five communication: truth, interest, and inspiration. (p. 135)

Resolution triptych. Three separate and definable peace. (p. 131)

Resolution. The speaker's lessening of audience tension. (p. 118)

Rhetoric of selfish power. Communication of the speaker's egotistic agenda and desire to control others. (p. 62)

Rhetoric of servanthood. Communication in which the speaker breaks the ego barrier and speaks on behalf of the hearers. (p. 62)

Sermo corporis. Communication through body-language. (p. 168)

Speech-before-the-speech. The speaker's first three minutes with the audience. During this time the speaker warms to the audience before beginning the formal talk. (p. 19)

Spiritual power. The *dynamis* God confers to empower the text in order to accomplish His purposes in His world. (p. 5)

Standby illustration file. A file of titled illustrations especially useful for guest speakers and leturers. (p. 199)

Tolkien's challenge. Leaving the audience with a happy ending. (p. 128)

Wrap, the. Speaker's closure of the communiqué that restates the promise, shows how he or she kept it, and asks listeners to firm up their response. (p. 104)